D0805535

Cather's Kitchens

Anna Pavelka, the model for the title character
of *My Ántonia,* posing with her birthday cake

By Roger L. and Linda K. Welsch

Foreword by Susan J. Rosowski

University of Nebraska Press: Lincoln and London

Cather's Kitchens

Foodways in Literature and Life

Copyright 1987 by the University of Nebraska Press
All rights reserved
Manufactured in the United States of America

The paper in this book meets the minimum requirements
of American National Standard for Information Sciences –
Permanence of Paper for Printed Library Materials,
ANSI Z39.48-1984.

Library of Congress Cataloging-in-Publication Data
Welsch, Roger L.
Cather's kitchens.
1. Cookery, American.   2. Nebraska – Social life and
customs.   3. Food habits – Nebraska.   4. Cather,
Willa, 1873-1947.   I. Welsch, Linda K.   II. Title.
TX715.W465   1987   394.1'09782   86-19148
ISBN 0-8032-4742-7 (alkaline paper)

HOUSTON PUBLIC LIBRARY

R0159036236
S S C

For the cooks in *our* lives, Bertha Welsch and Jake Hotovy

Contents

ILLUSTRATIONS

By Susan J. Rosowski

Foreword

In *Cather's Kitchens* Roger and Linda Welsch tell of learning from Willa Cather and others the traditions that govern plains cookery. They include recipes, sometimes complete with precise measurements. More important, they tell stories, suggesting by them the things not named that Claude Wheeler sensed in a kitchen he visited: "the fragrance of old friendships, the glow of early memories, belief in wonder-working rhymes and songs" (*One of Ours*, 1922; New York: Knopf, 1979, 45).

As is fitting for a conversation in a kitchen, the Welsches' manner is personal, casual, familiar. From it we learn about the Welsches—their love for their subject and their respect for its place in their daily lives. From it we learn too about Cather's writing, for the kitchen, a neglected setting in criticism on Cather, provides a fitting entry to it.

It is fitting too that Roger and Linda Welsch concentrate upon plains kitchens, for in them Cather learned her most important lessons in storytelling and in cooking. When newly arrived in Nebraska and feeling such homesickness for Virginia that she resolved to eat little (she didn't like canned foods anyway) until she returned to Virgina and fresh mutton, nine-year-old Willa Cather found comfort in farm kitchens, where she would spend a morning with one of the neighboring immigrant women at her baking or butter-making: "even when they spoke very little English, the old women somehow managed to tell me a great many stories about the old country"

(*The Kingdom of Art: Willa Cather's First Principles and Critical Statements, 1893–1896,* 1966).

Storytelling and food—the two are inseparable in Cather's fiction. *Cather's Kitchens* introduces both. After reading it (and it is a cookbook to be read, with recipes nestled in anecdote and story), we think of foods more nearly as Cather wrote of them. "Preparation of food is one of the most important things in life," Cather believed (*Willa Cather in Person,* UNP, 1987, 83. Hereafter cited as WCIP). A fine meal offers pleasure in the food and also in all that accompanies it—the tradition of the dish, the harmony of good company, and the excitement of the stories told with the meal.

Cather's Kitchens evokes interest too in the place of food and plains cooking within the broader spectrum of her canon. Within that spectrum the fiction preceding *My Ántonia* seems a prelude. There are memorable descriptions of food in the barn dance scene of "The Bohemian Girl" and in passages telling of Mrs. Bergson's near mania for preserving in *O Pioneers!*; yet in her early plains fiction Cather concentrated upon the relationship between immigrants and the land, and kitchens are an adjunct to that relationship. Alexandra Bergson expresses herself best not in the kitchen, which is occupied first by her mother and later by the pretty young Swedish girls who did her housework, but in the soil. *My Ántonia,* the novel that came most directly out of Cather's childhood in Nebraska, is a different matter altogether, for in it food is central.

As Cather described her introduction to the plains, so she described that of Jim Burden, her narrator in *My Ántonia.* The book opens and closes with kitchens—first his grandmother's underground one to which the ten-year-old Jim comes, then Ántonia Cuzak's, to which the middle-aged Jim returns. As Cather described her childhood feelings in terms of food, so in *My Ántonia* she wrote about food, like Nebraska's cornfields, as "one of the great economic facts . . . which underlie all the activities of men, in peace or war" (*My Ántonia,* 1918; Houghton Mifflin, Sentry Edition, 1961, 137. Hereafter cited as MA). Three of its five sections present three stages—acts even—of food production: wresting crops from a wild land; establishing a community to provide those crops to the world; creating a secure home in a productive country.

My Ántonia tells first of the plight of first generation immigrants in an alien land. People threatened with starvation give the closest attention to food, item by item, and in telling of homesteaders' early years in Nebraska Cather describes food with appropriate specificity. She lists provisions taken by Mrs. Burden to the Shimerdas—a sack of potatoes, a piece of cured pork, a jar of butter, some loaves of bread, several pumpkin pies—and she itemizes the food remaining in the Shimerda cave—a few frozen potatoes and a little pile of flour—at the time of Mrs. Burden's later visit that first hard winter. Cather also details foods served in the Burden household, their quantity a reassuring sign of security: chicken on Sunday, ham or bacon or sausage on other days, and an unending supply of pies and cakes. As Jim recalled, "Our lives centred around warmth and food" (MA, 66).

The second part of *My Ántonia,* "The Hired Girls," explodes with activity in response to an awakened plains. As if Kansas and Nebraska were enclosed and the temperature regulated by a thermometer, cornfields enlarged and multiplied, "until they would be, not the Shimerdas' cornfields, or Mr. Bushy's, but the world's cornfields" (MA, 137). In Black Hawk, the community that exists to link those cornfields to the world, kitchens bustle with activity—in Mrs. Harling's preserving was a prolonged festival, and there too Ántonia was at the center of an unending party. Finally, however, food production on such a scale cannot be contained within single homes; all of Black Hawk is devoted to it. As if from one gigantic kitchen, the smell of suppers cooking fills the air on winter evenings, that of buttered popcorn on spring afternoons. The farms surrounding the town seem an immense garden, with people moving from one to tend the other. Farm girls work in Black Hawk "to pay for ploughs and reapers, brood-sows, or steers to fatten" (MA, 200), and Mr. Harling leaves town to travel along his chain of elevators on the railroad that connects the cornfields to the world.

Jim Burden's return to Ántonia Cuzak in the final section is a return to the peace of a home in a productive land, to the kitchen and its extensions, the orchard and the fruit cellar. Here food is a spiritual reality rather than an economic fact, as it was in the Black Hawk section. It represents, as Roger and Linda Welsch discuss, love. Jim meets Ántonia again in her kitchen; from there she takes him to the orchard she and her husband have tended so carefully, and tells him of the trees that she thought of as children and that now yield the fruit stored in the family's new cellar. Days end with suppers over which Ántonia presides, passing food down the rows of children and, always, telling stories.

As a farmer's wife cooking for her large family, enjoying it and doing it well, Ántonia is an artist by Cather's terms. Not surprisingly, Cather described food in her plains writing with as much attention to aesthetic detail as that given to the exhibition of any work of art. At a barn dance, open doors frame a scene and golden light illuminates Johanna Vavrika, displaying to "the admiring women her platters heaped with fried chicken, her roasts of beef, boiled tongues, and baked hams with cloves stuck in the crisp brown fat and garnished with tansy and parsley" ("The Bohemian Girl," *Willa Cather's Collected Short Fiction*, 1892–1912, rev. ed., 1970. Hereafter cited as BG). A fruit cellar contains shelves of glass jars, gleaming like gems, and Ántonia's children shyly "traced on the glass with their finger-tips the outline of the cherries and strawberries and crab-apples within, trying by a blissful expression of countenance to give . . . some idea of their deliciousness" (MA, 338). As if for an unveiling, Mrs. Rosen wraps within a napkin her "symmetrically plaited coffee-cake, beautifully browned, delicately peppered over with poppy seeds, with sugary margins about the twists" (*Obscure Destinies*, 1932; Random House, Vintage Books, 1974, 76).

In her descriptions of plains kitchens Cather rejoiced in the abundance provided by an awakened land: "the mountains of food" cooked by a fine company of farm wives (BG); the vast supplies of meats, pies, and cakes Mrs. Burden prepares for the hungry men each day; the great quantities of sugar Antonia uses when preserving. Kitchens are a hub of activity, filled with the warmth of a cookstove, the smells of breads baking or fowl roasting, the sounds of people talking.

Because they so soon became rare, such kitchens take on added value in retrospect. In *One of Ours* and *A Lost Lady* Cather wrote of the disintegration of pioneer values as a weakening of the kitchen's place in the center of peoples' lives. The Wheeler home contains neither a heroic Alexandra presiding over her kitchen nor a mythic Ántonia at the center of hers; instead the good-hearted but simple-minded Mahailey tends the hearth, watching that Mrs. Wheeler re-members to eat and that Ralph Wheeler doesn't raid her pantry. Cather uses one of her last plains kitchens as the setting for the final disillusionment in *A Lost Lady.* The shyster lawyer Ivy Peters has taken possession of the Forrester property and of Mrs. Forrester too. When he places his hands over Mrs. Forrester's breasts as she uncon-cernedly stands working at the sink, his action seems doubly re-prehensible because it occurs in a room so closely associated with family.

As progress brings larger houses with more rooms, kitchens fade into the background, then disappear. In *The Professor's House* the St. Peters apologize for the slowness of service at a dinner in their new house, explaining that the kitchen (which is never seen) is not yet connected by wiring to the dining room. And in *My Mortal Enemy* the Henshawes live the last days of their marriage in a shabby boardinghouse, where Oswald prepares food on a hot plate or brings it in from a commercial kitchen.

With progress too, quantity, so celebrated in the pioneer nov-els, threatens to overwhelm. When a vast array of goods may be purchased readily at a grocery, discerning taste is necessary to reject the vulgar and protect that which is fine. Beginning with *The Pro-fessor's House,* Cather wrote positively about refined taste and select meals. Godfrey St. Peter is Cather's first gourmet, *The Professor's House* her first novel to offer French culture as an alternative, not to escape American materialism (as in *One of Ours*), but to exist within it. Offended by the vulgar consumption about him, St. Peter feels satisfaction in his walled French garden and his solitary Christmas lunch. The menu suggests how far Cather has come from the robust meals of her plains novels: chicken sandwiches with lettuce leaves, red California grapes, and two shapely long-necked russet pears. In *The Professor's House* meals with many people and much food are unhappy occasions; those meals presented positively are balanced, harmonious, and, especially, restrained. During a summer when his wife and daughter were in California and he was his own cook, St. Peter each morning walked to the market, where he "had his pick of the fruits and salads. He dined at eight o'clock. When he cooked a fine leg of lamb, *saignant,* well rubbed with garlic before it went into the pan, then he asked Outland to dinner. Over a dish of steaming asparagus, swathed in a napkin to keep it hot, they talked and watched night fall in the garden" (*The Professor's House,* 1925; Random House, Vintage Books, 1973, 176).

Death Comes for the Archbishop offers a vast array of foods and meals. Two French missionaries, Fathers Latour and Vaillant, learn about the people living in the American Southwest by eating their food, sitting at their tables, and hearing there the stories of their lives: the simple grace of Latour's meal with Jacinto, his Indian guide; the slovenly table of Father Martínez, who feeds cats carelessly from his plate; the tyranny of Friar Baltazar, who killed a serving boy for spilling a sauce. Food, always an index to character in Cather's fiction, makes dramatic the contrasting, yet complementary personalities of Fathers Latour and Vaillant. Prepared by Vaillant, a Christmas dinner brings France close to the two priests. Ritual surrounds the meal: the candles lighting the table, the grace beginning the meal, the appreciative silence upon tasting the onion soup. Humor climaxes the scene. Latour understands what the soup represents and, pushing his chair back, reflects that it is "not the work of one man. It is the result of a constantly refined tradition. There are nearly a thousand years of history in this soup." Vaillant, frowning intently at the brown soup pot, declares it is leeks that interest him, that king of vegetables without which a man cannot make a proper soup (*Death Comes for the Archbishop,* 1927; Random House, Vintage Books, 1971, 38–40).

In *Shadows on the Rock,* her late novel about immigrants to a far land, Cather again made the kitchen her central setting, this time including her most developed philosophy surrounding it. Her story is of the instruction of twelve-year-old Cécile Auclair in domestic ritual, by which a kitchen is made a safe haven from a threatening wilderness. More than Cather's other novels, *Shadows on the Rock* is filled with descriptions of meals rather than of separate foods; it is Cather's most extended tribute to the French ability to "build a menu as an artistic and scientific composition of perfect balance" (wcip, 83). Cécile Auclair prepares for Father Hector a fish soup, followed by wood doves cooked in a casserole with mushrooms and served with wild rice; with it they drink a fine old Burgundy. A dinner party consists of "a dish made of three kinds of shell-fish, a *tête de veau,* . . . a roast capon with a salad, and for dessert Breton pancakes with honey and preserves" (*Shadows on the Rock,* 1931; Random House, Vintage Books, 1971, 216. Hereafter cited as sor).

Menus here are different from meals in Cather's plains novels, most surely. But the epiphany Cather gives to Cécile Auclair applies to cooking of all kinds. After Cécile returns from visiting a family living in semibarbarism, she reenters her own kitchen newly conscious of what it means to her: "These coppers, big and little, these brooms and clouts and brushes, were tools; and with them one made, not shoes or cabinet-work, but life itself. One made a climate within a climate; one made the days,—the complexion, the special flavour, the special happiness of each day as it passed; one made life" (sor, 197–98).

Preface

This book is in some ways an apology to Robert Knoll. He taught my freshman English class. Not me, but my freshman English class. It's not as if he didn't try to teach me. He offered the class new books and old classics; he praised and damned, entertained and outraged, but I had more important things on my mind. Hormones, I think. At any rate, he offered us Willa Cather's *My Ántonia,* and I didn't understand. I still may not understand, but I am a damned sight closer than I was thirty years ago. Now when I read Cather, I understand mostly how heroic Robert Knoll's patience was in not simply clubbing me to death and giving up.

Now Cather's books leave me voiceless, wordless. I find those nuances Professor Knoll (although we are now colleagues, I cannot to this day call him anything but Professor Knoll) tried to lead me to all those years ago. I could regret that I didn't find it all then so that I could have had these intervening decades to think about it, but I would rather rejoice that I have found what I have in the interim.

It may seem strange to be offering a book about that mundane, inelegant peasant pursuit of cooking in terms of Willa Cather, that literary star who hobnobbed with the Menuhins and was the toast of Europe and all that. Well, my reading is that Willa Cather was a woman, a peasant at heart, a Nebraskan, a plainswoman—and a cook. Better yet, an eater. Perhaps as much a gourmand as a gourmet.

That may be our own prejudice and our own preference. We'll

accept that judgment. God knows, plenty of others have done with Cather what they have wanted to do, whatever the facts seem to suggest.

Of course time and distance and refinement honed Cather's tastes in food as they did her tastes in music and literature. When she vacationed in Red Cloud she could, as described by Edith Lewis in *Willa Cather Living: A Personal Record* (Lincoln: University of Nebraska Press, 1976), spend "a great deal of time" cooking pies, cookies, and puddings and travel from Bohemian homestead to Danish homestead to Norwegian homestead sampling wild-plum wine, but her later life was characterized by more elegant foods, although deliberately selected foods.

Even though Lewis has Cather in the 1930s being urbanely cosmopolitan—"garlic and olive oil from New York, bread from Montreal, wild strawberry jam from Quebec; and shipments every week from an excellent grocer in St. John"—Cather remains the fundamental cook: "With these we were able to break the monotony of our fare with splendid banquets, cooked on a little wood-burning range."

In *Willa Cather: A Memoir* (Lincoln: University of Nebraska Press, 1967), Elizabeth Shepley Sergeant has Cather in the 1920s becoming a demanding diner, if not a snob ("She insisted on the tarragon."), dining at Delmonico's and generally being the kind of guest who causes waiters' eyes to roll up in their heads. But Sergeant also reports that when Cather was discussing the Scandinavian translations of *O Pioneers!* with Alvin Johnson, "all they managed to talk about was food!"

We suppose that just as everyone has his price, everyone has his amount of time in New York or London sufficient to destroy decency, and we don't doubt that with Cather's success and Cather's ego she may indeed have come to accept that standard of obnoxiousness accepted in New York as normal; so when we read something like Sergeant's memoir, we prefer to ascribe paragraphs like the following to the boorishness that comes inevitably from breathing the air of the city:

Bring tea that is hot, HOT, H O T, she ordered the table waiter. Brioche, petits fours, a Napoleon, two babas au rhum. And—with a prick of her porcupine quills that set him scuttling off—the BEST China tea, strong and delicate.

We prefer to seek that part of her that was Nebraskan, that part, perhaps, that is revealed in Sergeant's very next paragraph:

"You're not superior to the sense of taste, are you?" Willa Cather inquired gaily. Sharing a good meal with her remained from this day forth one of life's serious pleasures. Conversation must never divert one from the quality of the food on the plate and the wine in the glass.

Whatever Cather's feelings about food, in her youth and in her maturity, it is abundantly clear to us that she uses it extensively as a literary device, and we have elected to devote this study to Cather's foods. It is our contention that she used them widely to develop characters, express region, and delineate ethnicity and that it is therefore useful in understanding Cather to understand her foods.

Moreover, writers like Cather, Mari Sandoz, and Wright Morris are successful in part because they are accurate observers and manage to portray their observations coherently to their readers. They have seen a culture in a historical context, have recorded it, and have transmitted it in a particularly powerful manner. The result is that their work can also be of use to ethnographers who want to understand better that time and place the authors have observed.

Cather saw pioneer kitchens and tasted foods at pioneer tables. Her tastes were educated at those tables as much as at her desk. They are therefore worth examining. It is our intention in this book to provide a new dimension to Cather scholarship, to open a new perspective on the plains pioneer, and to recall some old foods that still might suit the modern palate.

Willa Cather grew up in a tradition that gave a good deal of importance to matters of food. The family's nineteenth-century letters are filled with talk about eggs, mutton, gardens, cherries, plums, pickles, and canning. Her own letters to Webster County from New York are focused notably on food. She lamented that whenever she was sick, she lost her favorite delight—her taste for food—and she remarked on January 20, 1945, that she was getting food poisoning from eating too often at hotels. In 1939 she wrote that she had stuffed a turkey for her brother Douglas because her French cook in New York couldn't do the job the way her grandmother had.

When she sent gifts of food to favorite friends, such as Annie Pavelka, she sent money to someone in Red Cloud to buy food there because she considered it so superior to the kinds of things she could find in New York. In 1934 she asked that specific foods from the cellars of her Red Cloud friends and relatives be sent over to other friends. She remembered and esteemed the inventories and specialties of those homely cellars a thousand miles from New York City.

Despite her reputation as one of the era's leading artists, in a letter dated May 16, 1941, she measured her friends and acquaintances as cooks and scholars—in that order! Cather used food as a gesture of love. She stated this explicitly in a letter written in 1922. And again despite her cosmopolitan life, her letters from the city delighted almost exclusively in the peasant, coarse fare of the Nebraska landscape—ham sandwiches, for example, and cold water from wooden pails.

In this effort we want to thank the Nebraska Committee for the Humanities for its support of our initial research for the project, especially Ann Cognard, who seemed so intent on helping us in our work. Ann Billesbach surprised us again and again by helping us not only when we asked but also by volunteering whatever she happened to run across that might serve our work. Ann Billesbach is a very special person, and our gratitude to her is sincere and profound.

Viola Borton helped us in the early stages of our research, seeking support and information, and John Carter, who has helped us with almost everything we have ever undertaken, was there yet once again when we needed him. Helping us with recipes were Ann Billesbach, Sally Hotovy, Jake Hotovy, Cherie Underwood,

Deb Novacek, Alice Styskal, Darlene Divis, Virginia Hoffbauer, Harriett Nielsen, Adeline Spicka, Bertha Welsch, Berniece Pelt, Mary Lambrecht, Viola Schumm, Emily Kresse, Anna Horacek, Jennie Miner Reiher, Helen Obitz, Dudley Bailey, and Bonnie Hueftle.

Finally, we want to thank Charles Cather, caretaker of Willa Cather's literary interests, for his kind permission to use the passages from Cather's works in this book.

All photographs are reproduced by courtesy of the Willa Cather Pioneer Memorial and Educational Foundation Collection and the Nebraska State Historical Society with the exception of the photograph of the Fourth Avenue Market in Red Cloud, Nebraska, which is reproduced by courtesy of the Nebraska State Historical Society.

The cooks, kitchens, and foods treated in this volume are from *One of Ours, My Ántonia*, "Neighbour Rosicky," and *O Pioneers!*. Because the references from those works are central to the purpose of this book, we have avoided using footnotes for citations and instead have inserted work and page citations in the text. Within the references we have abbreviated as follows:

One of Ours = OO
My Ántonia = MA
"Neighbor Rosicky" = NR
O Pioneers! = OP

Page numbers are from the following editions of the works:

My Ántonia (Boston: Houghton Mifflin Company, n.d., Sentry Edition 7

One of Ours (New York: Vintage Books, 1971)

O Pioneers! (Boston: Houghton Mifflin Company, n.d., Sentry Edition 16

"Neighbour Rosicky," in *Five Stories* (New York: Vintage Books, 1956)

Other sources of information about Plains pioneer cookery are Roger Welsch's *Treasury of Nebraska Pioneer Folklore* (Lincoln: University of Nebraska Press, 1966) and *Sod Walls* (Broken Bow, Nebr.: Purcells, 1968), and Kay Graber's *Nebraska Pioneer Cookbook* (Lincoln: University of Nebraska Press, 1974).

Wherever we have inserted our own words, observations, or substitutions for the words of Cather or a recipe text or any other text, we have placed my contribution in brackets: [ ]. When we are writing our mutual opinions or experience, we have used the plural pronoun *we.* Wherever the text reads *I,* it is specifically Roger Welsch's words; Linda's passages are identified with her name.

This effort is not meant to be an examination of Cather's writing but rather of her use of foodways within her writing. We think it would be inappropriate therefore to spend much time dealing with the stories or characterizations within the novels and the short story we are dealing with here. We hope this book will be of use and interest to people who have never read Willa Cather and to those who have read but not enjoyed her work. Obviously, this book should be of substantially greater interest to someone who does enjoy Cather, and the meaning of the foods dealt with here will be much more interesting and meaningful to that person who has read the works we have drawn on, especially if the reading has been recent. We strongly recommend that you read this book, or use it as a cookbook, with *My Ántonia, O Pioneers!, One of Ours,* and "Neighbour Rosicky" well in mind, if not in hand.

ROGER L. WELSCH
LINDA K. WELSCH

Frontier Foods

> There seemed to be nothing to see; no fences, no creeks or trees, no hills or fields. If there was a road, I could not make it out in the faint starlight. There was nothing but land: not a country at all, but the material out of which countries are made. No, there was nothing but land. . . . (MA 7)

It is hard for us to imagine today what the plains were like for the new migrants. Perhaps it is impossible. Everything they had known as life and culture was gone—the language and dress, forest and fjords, mountains and sea. Gone were the pleasant villages of Czechoslovakia and France, where the church bells of the neighboring villages could be heard on a Sunday morning. Gone were the fine old buildings of brick, stone, and logs. Gone the roads that had been traveled since the Romans built them. Gone the good wines and beer. The old folksongs lost their meaning here on the plains, and the folktales too, for who could imagine a witch's gingerbread house sitting in the middle of the Nebraska grasslands?

Of course gone too were the oppressive petty tyrants, serfdom, perpetual poverty, and the eternal wars of central and northern Europe. The new advantages of hope for peace and prosperity were more than enough to compensate for the hardships of life on the Great Plains, but those hardships remained.

If logs and stone were not available, they would live in houses of sod. If the neighbors were Dutch and Greek, then Norwegian would be forgotten and they would take up the language of their new homeland. If they could not have the annual forty inches of rainfall they could expect on the Oder River, then they would pray for twenty here on the Republican. Instead of cod, they would settle for an occasional catfish.

Perhaps the hardest change for the new plainsmen to make was at the supper table. The Germans have a proverb, *Man ist, was man isst* ("We are what we eat"), and that is more than a metaphor. Food is far more than nourishment. It can be a symbol of success or failure, wealth or poverty, civilization or savagery. Food can be a link with a time past or a future prayed for.

In a way, all food is soul food. It is a cultural expression, and every bite, every meal, recharges memories and prejudices about food and culture. Some food is sacred, some profane; some foods bring tears of joy and gratitude, while others are eaten only under severe duress—and those reactions have little to do with the taste of the food. The plains required all manner of adjustment to food and cooking, changes that shook families and communities to their very roots.

Imagine, for example, the dilemma of the migrant Norwegian family arriving in America in 1872 and settling somewhere in central Nebraska. Their lives have been totally disrupted. Now they face hazards and problems they never imagined in their worst dreams in the Old Country: prairie fires moving faster than a man could ride on horseback, Indian raids, grasshopper storms, murderous hail that could drop livestock in the pastures, heat and cold beyond their experience, half the rainfall they would have expected at home. Everything had changed, in field and town, house and barn.

And what of the kitchen? Well, in the fields the man of the family was at least still using a plow and horse, even if the field was ten times the size of the fields he had worked in the homeland. The home still had walls, even if they were sod, and a roof, even if it too was of sod and leaked.

But the kitchen. Oh, the kitchen! Nothing was the same here, nothing. In the Old Country all cooking had been done in a stone or brick fireplace and bake oven; wood was an abundant resource. All "recipes" (I must use quotation marks because the word suggests a written formula, while in Europe recipes were rarely written down, and if they were, they did not usually include proportions) were known in terms of a wood fire and its peculiarities; bread depended on the radiant heat of a wood-fired bake oven. The plains withheld from the pioneer housewife precisely those two things necessary to her kitchen: stone and wood. For the men in the fields it was a joy not to have to stumble over the incessant stones and tree roots that they had fought for centuries in Norway, Germany, Vermont, or Indiana, but for the women in the kitchen the situation was desperate. They had to learn all over again how to cook, using a cast-iron stove. They did, and they learned to cook as well or better with the iron stove than they had with the fireplace.

And fuel. Here trees were so rare they had names. How many women, I wonder, looked around them and wept with despair, wondering how they were going to cook for their children where there were no trees. Once again the plains answered the question with a joke that brought forth little laughter: women who had weekly scrubbed their kitchens to dazzling white, for whom cleanliness was second to godliness only by a very narrow margin, were to cook with manure.

In the Old Country the cows had been trained not to soil even their barn stalls, so that the barn, although it might be under the same roof as the family's living quarters, was immaculate, and now, here in this Nebraska place, the manure from the pastures and fields was to be picked up by hand and carried into the house. To cook food.

But there was no choice, and so it was.

Quickly women learned that cowchips were a clean and efficient fuel and some cooks changed to cobs only when the cowchips were used up. Whether they used cowchips or cobs, whole corn or sunflower stalks, or even "cats" of twisted grass for fuel, the women brought their new cooking skills to the edge of art, so that from the newfangled stoves, with unaccustomed fuels, there were soon fine cakes and breads that might just as well have come from the old stone fireplace ovens fired with good clean Norwegian spruce.

So the migrant cooks found that when they reached the Great American Desert they had to use new heat sources and new cooking tools. It was not simply a matter of using cobs and cookstoves to cook the foods they and their mothers and their mothers' mothers had cooked for as long as anyone could remember. For the Norwegians there was no cod for *lutefisk,* for the Germans no barley for beer or grapes for wine, for the Greeks no nuts for *baklava.* Moreover, with many families—even when supplies for traditional foods were available—Old World foods were sometimes rejected by paternal declaration: "We are now Americans, and we will wear American shoes, and we will speak American, and we will eat American food too. This country has adopted us and now we will adopt it."

Thus, in many households, in many neighborhoods and communities, the old foods became a matter of embarrassment. For many Europeans peasant food was part and parcel of a life they had rejected and left behind, so the food was removed from the day-to-day table and made an appearance only at holiday festivities, where it could be served as a modest, respectable reminder of the past (where it now baffles many a European visitor who finds "rich" Americans eating for major annual feasts the lowliest of peasant foods: *lutefisk* and *lefsa* for Christmas, *Schnitzsupp* and *Grebel* on Good Friday).

The two world wars contributed to the pressures against ethnic foodways on the plains. Foreign languages—Danish and Czech as well as German—were held in contempt and suspicion by the 1,000 percent Americans. Families who maintained an ethnic kitchen no longer were embarrassed by their cultural conservatism but found themselves in very real physical danger from patriotic zealots.

Other families clung tenaciously to the old ways because they remained to them the right ways. In large communities, where there was safety in numbers, or on isolated farmsteads, where they could be overlooked, housewives continued to bake their *kolaches* and *bliny,* brewed duck-blood soups and *kvass.*

Plains foodways were therefore subject to three major influences in pioneer years, and all three of these elements can be found in
Cather's treatments of plains foods, even though the periods she
writes about are more accurately thought of as settlement than frontier: ethnic survivals; eastern American foodways; new foodways
developing on the Great Plains as a direct result of the historic and
geographic demands of the region.

Indian foodways had surprisingly little impact on migrant
food patterns. Nobody molds easily into a totally new food system
in any event, but here the problems of borrowing foodways from
the Indians were more in number and more complex than mere cultural inertia.

For one thing, by the time non-Indian peoples began invading
and occupying what is now the Great Plains there was already the
understanding and presumption that relations between the migrants
and the native plainsmen—Ponca, Kiowa, Oto, Sioux, Cheyenne,
and Arapaho—would be cool and guarded at best, more often outright hostile, so there was little opportunity for the kind of com-
munication that leads to the exchange and adoption of another culture's foodways.

During times of great famine there is ample evidence that pioneers did turn to Indian foods—to edible wild plants, for example,
that we generally do not include in either European or American
foodways and to cooking and preservation techniques, such as the
drying of beef and game, and most accounts make it abundantly
clear that Indian foods and cookery were considered to be quite
good. Yet when the famine had passed, the pioneer diet unerringly
returned to the American or ethnic fare that had been there before,
without a sign left in the general menu that Indian food had ever
been sampled, yet appreciated. (See Roger Welsch, "American
Plains Indian Ethnogastronomy," *Ethnologische Nahrungsforschung,*
Helsinki, 1975, or "Sorry Chuck: Pioneer Foodways," *Nebraska
History,* 53:1, Spring, 1972).

It appears that the pioneers rejected Indian foods and cooking
techniques which they acknowledged to be good and nutritious,
which were more convenient and reliable than their own foodways.

We might well ask why. Because, comes the sad answer, Indian food was considered to be low class. We can hear a pioneer homesteader say, "Why, what a humiliation it would be for the Johnsons to drop by and find us eating INDIAN food! What would they think?"

Of course the same thing is true today too: many of the weeds we hold in such great contempt on the plains are considered crops and groceries in other parts of the world. Dandelions are cursed in Nebraska and grown as a crop in Massachusetts; Americans who fight groundcherries in their gardens pay premium prices for them as Hawaiian "poha" jelly. And some things we consider to be food are elsewhere regarded as trash: Europeans are aghast when they see Americans eating pig food: corn on the cob. A few changes in history and Nebraska might have been known as the Milkweed State or the Groundcherry Capital of the World.

Some of the foods enjoyed by the pioneers and depicted by Cather seem to the modern reader or cook to be plain and uninspired, but bear in mind first of all that any variety at all in diet was considered a major event; an orange at Christmas would be savored and anticipated for weeks until Mother finally insisted that it be eaten because it was the only orange a child might see for the entire year. Second, foods are often far better than their names, recipes, or reputations suggest. Today we are victims of foodways prejudices as crippling as any in the world. Canned pork and beans, for example, cannot hold a candle to home-cured sowbelly and fresh beans—standard pioneer fare that is so good my mouth waters at the thought of it but which by its name leads the modern eater, no matter how hungry, to conjure up thoughts of graceless gruels. What we have come to think of as pork and beans is at best a pale shadow of the original.

This letter, sent to me by Myrtle Oxford Hersh, says a good deal about pioneer foods and attitudes toward food:

I can't call up adjectives to describe the super quality of [corn] bread when eaten with "cow butter" or ham gravy, with a glass or two of rich milk or buttermilk made in the old wooden churn. It was simply "out of this world," as the youngsters would say today. So while we did not have frosted cakes, pies with two inches of meringue, and many other musts of today, we had food which met the needs of growing, healthy bodies and we did not have to keep a bottle of vitamins from A to Z to keep us in good health.

After a night of sound sleep we would be awakened in the morning to the tune of the coffee mill grinding the coffee for breakfast, or Mother sharpening her butcher knife on the stovepipe or a stoneware crock as she prepared to slice ham, bacon or venison for breakfast as an accompaniment to hot butter-milk biscuits, potatoes, or fried mush, which made a real meal on which to start a strenuous day. (sw, p. 146)

So, as you try the recipes from this book, be they frontier foods or the foods from Cather's works, keep in mind the context in which they were prepared and consumed. As you sample them, cast away as much as possible of your twentieth-century supermarket culture. Try to imagine catching a quick supper while bedding down the animals and greasing the wagon in preparation for another long day of eight miles' travel across this desert called Nebraska Territory. Conjure up images of a blizzard howling outside your sod-house windows as you gratefully sit down to a dish of corn mush and fatback. Think of the bustle of Ántonia's kitchen and the love that she put into her *kolaches* as a basic ingredient.

Eventually the Oregon Trail, Mormon Trail, and Texas Trail passed and people began to see Nebraska as a place to live in rather than simply to travel through. Some of them ran out of money— could not go on, could not go back—and so they became plains- men. In other cases a member of the family died along the trail of snakebite, cholera, or the most common cause of injury and death on the Oregon Trail, accidental gunshot wound; the rest of the family simply could not go on and leave the one member behind beneath the prairie sod, so they stayed.

Others came here seeking gold. Not the kind of gold you might find in the streams and rocks of Colorado and California, but the kind that grows on a cob.

As the frontier passed and as we enter the world of Cather's cookery, things changed. There were grocery stores in towns like Red Cloud, and drastic shortages of fuels, ingredients (other than some ethnic items), and cooking utensils were no longer the problem they had been on the frontier. But the memories of those hard times were still there. Perhaps that is precisely why Cather has made so much of foods in her works.

In Cather's works the ethnic memories were still strong enough that there are strange-sounding names of unlikely dishes, and yet settlement is complete enough that the pioneers had developed the new dishes that were purely "American." And there were the dishes that long had been considered of this new land. There are no cowboys, no Indians, no Oregon Trailers, but the memories of their accumulated foodways knowledge has not been lost on the settlers who followed. Cather captures that spirit.

All of the channels of these rivers of food came together on Cather's prairie. The echoes of ethnic foods are strong in her works, and the rural atmosphere in her menus. Now that we have explored the table of the frontier soddie, we can turn to the next stage: Cather's kitchens.

Cather's Kitchens

> Mrs. Wheeler always feels that God is near,—but Mahailey is not troubled by any knowledge of interstellar spaces, and for her He is nearer still,—directly overhead, not so very far above the kitchen stove. (OO, 391)

Cather's kitchens come from the period when the landscape had been settled but was not yet fully understood, when the inhabitants were still homesteaders, but ones who had plowed their fields many springs. They were no longer bringing all of their foodstuffs from the East but they were still not altogether certain what it was that would grow in their gardens. There were no more open fireplaces, no dirt floors, but the dishes, the meals, and the kitchens could be seen to be distinctly plains. The hosts and the guests are all Americans, but they are still close enough to their origins that the foods are known by their Czech, French, or German names and retain whatever flavor possible of the Old World. There is plenty of food in most of Cather's kitchens, but the memory of hunger is vivid enough that food is prized and respected.

While the villages of Cather's environment—Bladen and Red Cloud, for example—were small, new, and crude by some standards, they were ferocious in their intent to grow, to be cultured, to be civilized. Because experiences had been harsh in so many cases and because expectations remained modest in terms of personal wealth, relatively modest meals and dishes were admired as opulent in the countryside, in the small towns, and on the farms. A good deal of food was grown by the consumers themselves and was therefore understood and respected by them.

It is naïve to think that the life of Cather's people was simpler than ours. The knowledge, time, and strength to grow one's own food, preserve it, prepare it, serve it required considerably more individual skills than our own open-the-can-and-add-the-water culture. Perhaps what leads us so frequently into that simple life error is the clear condition that such a life was quieter and more satisfying.

Cather's cooks were in control of their kitchens and their foods. They may not have been able to obtain all that they wanted by way of supplies or precisely the variety or quality they wanted, but they knew what they had, they knew that its eventual value was up to them and them alone, and that sense of being in control of one's circumstances simply cannot be underestimated.

Grace at a pioneer plains table was said, we suspect, with particular intensity and sincerity. Food was a gift of grace, regardless of its humility, and the gift was always welcome.

One of the reasons that Willa Cather's works are so widely recognized as superior literature, and one of the reasons that her works are so widely ignored by general readers, is that a primary characteristic of her writing is subtlety. She is sometimes described as humorless, and yet it is precisely her humor that we find so attractive. It is difficult indeed to ignore the marvelous sting, for example, of passages like that in *One of Ours* where Cather makes clear her understanding of what kinds of people become professors:

"Julius is going abroad to study this fall. He intends to be a professor."

"What's the matter with him? Does he have poor health?" (oo 79)

Or her understanding about where the healthy climates are. In *My Ántonia* she has Gaston Cleric reversing the normal convention, leaving the Mediterranean and coming to the Great Plains for his health:

He came West at the suggestion of his physicians, his health having been enfeebled by a long illness in Italy. (MA 257)

Or what sorts of wisdom reside in the minds of the innocent as they watch the peregrinations of the sophisticated:

> Mahailey . . . [watched the wedding ceremony closely] in order to miss nothing. . . . she hoped to catch some visible sign of the miracle he was performing. She always wondered just what it was the preacher did to make the wrongest thing in the world the rightest thing in the world. (OO 165)

Cather is not so subtle about her attitudes toward food. She leaves no doubt about how she feels about country food as opposed to city food, about what a kitchen should be or inevitably must be, or about what the cook's relationship is to the food he or she prepares and to the people who eat that food.

In *O Pioneers!* she writes:

The pleasantest rooms in the house are the kitchen—where Alexandra's three young Swedish girls chatter and cook and pickle and preserve all summer long—and the sitting-room. . . . (OP 84)

> Next to getting warm and keeping warm, dinner and supper were the most interesting things we had to think about. Our lives centred around warmth and food and the return of the men at nightfall. (MA 66)

In *My Ántonia* Cather's protagonist and alter ego Jim Burden tells us:

I went softly down to the kitchen which, tucked away so snugly underground, always seemed to me the heart and centre of the house. (MA 101)

Anyone who has experienced a plains winter evening in a farm home will understand with marvelously sympathetic vibrations the image of that latter kitchen:

There, on the bench behind the stove, I thought and thought about Mr. Shimerda. Outside I could hear the wind singing over hundreds of miles of snow. It was as if I had let the old man in out of the tormenting winter, and were sitting there with him. (MA 101)

As we shall explore in more detail in a few pages, Cather's kitchens, like most rural kitchens, are far more than places where food is prepared. In most homes, then as now, the kitchen was where food was also eaten, the dining room—if there was one— being reserved for very special occasions like weddings, or visits from the minister, or perhaps when the governor dropped by. It can thus be imagined that dining rooms served primarily as hallways between the kitchen and the living room or as hallowed areas where echoes remained of a civilization that once was fervently anticipated but which was rarely realized.

The kitchen served as the rural reading room (OP 31) and the room where baths were taken (MA 9–10). It was the greenhouse for the mistress of the kitchen, where she nurtured plants that could serve not only as spice for her foods and medicine for her family but also as color and perfume for her life on the plains, which might otherwise be devoid of color and perfume.

We must again stress however that the kitchens, cooks, and foods that we are treating here are *rural* or at least *small town*. For all of the sophistication and culture that is attributed to Cather, we prefer to think of her as an Ántonia at heart, still the peasant yearn- ing for the warmth of a farm kitchen cluttered with children and hired hands. Cather again and again uses food as a symbol of things that are good and bad food—or too little food—as a symbol of what is bad. The same is true of kitchens. Rural kitchens are good; urban kitchens are bad. It is that simple:

On starlight nights I used to pace up and down those long, cold streets, scowling at the little, sleeping houses on either side, with their storm- windows and covered back porches. They were flimsy shelters, most of them poorly built of light wood, with spindle porch-posts horribly muti- lated by the turning-lathe. Yet for all their frailness, how much jealousy and envy and unhappiness some of them managed to contain! The life that went on in them seemed to me made up of evasions and negations; shifts to save cooking, to save washing and cleaning, devices to propitiate the tongue of gossip. This guarded mode of existence was like living under a tyranny. People's speech, their voices, their very glances, became furtive and re- pressed. Every individual taste, every natural appetite, was bridled by caution. The people asleep in those houses, I thought, tried to live like the mice in their own kitchens; to make no noise, to leave no trace, to slip over the surface of things in the dark. (MA 219)

The furniture of Cather's kitchens is not thoroughly inventoried in her writing, perhaps because the kitchen is always such a matter of fact. That may account in large part for that room's role in the stability of a house and family, not only in Cather's works but in the reality of each one of us even today. Front rooms may become living rooms and parlors may be renamed family rooms, and sofas may become couches or love seats or recliners, and chairs may become ottomans or beanbags, but a kitchen and its complements remain pretty much the same, not heeding the winds of fashion. One needs a stove, cupboards, tables, and chairs.

In the days of Cather's cooks the stove was perhaps more imposing than it is today. The cookstove with nickel and enamel cosmetics, gleaming black cooking surfaces, reservoir on one side, stoking doors on the other, concentric lids, draft and damper (or dampner as it was so often called), and warming ovens, doors on sides, front, and top, grates, grills, and levers. It all seems so imposing to the modern cook that it is dismissed as primitive and impractical.

Two proofs deny that suggestion: I cannot even guess at the number of Wisconsin, Minnesota, Dakota, and Nebraska homes I have visited where the old cookstove still occupies an important, almost revered, position in the household (albeit perhaps in a summer kitchen or basement) because some things simply cannot be cooked on anything other than a cookstove. Curiously, that food that requires the old cookstove's special heat is an ethnic dish— perhaps a German sausage or Czech *kolache*—or a dish that is particularly important for a festival like Christmas. One gets the very clear impression that the cookstove lends more to its products than heat.

The second proof that the old cookstove is more than a primitive expedient is that the modern cook takes a long time to learn the technology of the cookstove. If it is so primitive and simple, why is it that it takes so much time and judgment to learn how to use it? If it is such a backward device, why are the stews that come from its top and the breads that come from its ovens so wonderfully superior?

As I entered the kitchen, I sniffed a pleasant smell of gingerbread baking. The stove was very large, with bright nickel trimmings, and behind it there was a long wooden bench against the wall, and a tin washtub, into which grandmother poured hot and cold water. (MA 9–10)

Nowhere does Cather describe a kitchen more warmly than she does in *My Ántonia* (MA 330–31), where the fulfilled Ántonia reigns as queen. This kitchen is my favorite and the most accurate ethnographic description of a kitchen of the period, I believe, because it carries with it the element of life, that dimension that no museum with exhibits behind glass and plastic can ever capture— the sounds of children, the smell of *kolaches* in the oven, that peculiar dry warmth that only a cookstove can give, the sound of the wood crackling, the faint hints of smoke and the shimmering of heat waves rising from the top of the range:

I looked through the wire screen into a big, light kitchen with a white floor. I saw a long table, rows of wooden chairs against the wall, and a shining range in one corner. Two girls were washing dishes at the sink, laughing and chattering, and a little one, in a short pinafore, sat on a stool playing with a rag baby. When I asked for their mother, one of the girls dropped her towel, ran across the floor with noiseless feet, and disappeared. (MA 330–31)

Where or when there was little wood, the cook would reach into the cob box, which always sat at the stoking end of the cookstove, or go out of the kitchen into the back yard to the shed where cobs were kept. A good cook always had her cob carrier with her:

Old Mahailey herself came in from the yard, with her apron full of corn-cobs to start a fire in the kitchen stove. (OO 3)

The pioneer cook's relationship with the cookstove has always struck me as a curious one. The stove's hunger is worse than a baby's and yet there is some substantial satisfaction in knowing that as long as one takes care of getting the cobs or kindling, the stove will always be warm, in contrast to our current gas or electric stoves, which can go out at any time for reasons that apparently depend on the whims of ogres or magnetic vibrations in Minnesota. Just as surely as a pioneer cursed those occasions when the flue didn't draw and the house filled with choking cob smoke, he or she returned again and again to that unforgettable joy of waking in the morning to the perfume of smoke rising to the loft and the sound of cast-iron lids being moved to make room for a frying pan:

> On the morning of the eighth of April Claude came downstairs early and began to clean his boots, which were caked with dry mud. Mahailey was squatting down beside her stove, blowing and puffing into it. The fire was always slow to start in heavy weather. . . .
>
> "Mr. Claude," Mahailey grumbled, "this stove ain't never drawed good like my old one Mr. Ralph took away from me. I can't do nothin' with it. Maybe you'll clean it out for me next Sunday."
>
> "I'll clean it today, if you say so. . . ." (OO 201)

It might be noted here too that there is still many an old-timer who maintains that that smokiness was one of the advantages of the old cookstove. Before you had stepped out the door you could tell precisely how the weather was going, as Mahailey herself notes in the passage above.

Mahailey, the old cook in *One of Ours*, is one of those people we so often encounter who though illiterate and uneducated, perhaps in this case a bit slow mentally, nonetheless again and again provide the wisdom that comes only out of simplicity. The young man of her family, Claude, is about to go to France to the trenches of World War I and she tries to grasp the enormity of that journey and that war. Her realm is her kitchen, and it is within that context that she understands even something as international as war, so much bigger than a kitchen and yet fundamentally never more clearly horrible to Mahailey than a destroyed kitchen:

> Over the flour barrel in the corner Mahailey had tacked a Red Cross poster; a charcoal drawing of an old woman poking with a stick in a pile of plaster and twisted timbers that had once been her home. Claude went over to look at it while he dried his hands.

"Where did you get your picture?"

"She's over there where you're goin', Mr. Claude. There she is, huntin' for somethin' to cook with; no stove nor no dishes nor nothin'—everything all broke up. I reckon she'll be mighty glad to see you comin'." (OO 217)

While writing *Sod Walls* I was often moved when I would pore over photographs of humble sod houses stuck in the middle of nowhere, coveys of barefoot children (often all dressed in material of the identical pattern and color, sewn by their mother from the same bolt of store-bought cloth), and a woman who was probably thirty but looked fifty, standing with her family here at the end of the earth. And behind her, in one of the windows, on a table outside the door, would be a collection of tin cans and buckets with plants in them. Cather's kitchens are no exception:

Up under the wooden ceiling there were little half-windows with white curtains, and pots of geraniums and wandering Jew in the deep sills." (MA 9)

While the boys were getting the Doctor's horse, he went to the window to examine the house plants. "What do you do to your geraniums to keep them blooming all winter, Mary? I never pass this house that from the road I don't see your windows full of flowers." (NR 78)

One must wonder all the more because such small joys as house plants required such constant efforts to maintain on the Great Plains of the nineteenth century. The single-glass windows of even the houses in a town like Red Cloud meant that whatever was close to them froze, and every night the plants had to be moved closer to the heat source or protected somehow from the bitter cold of the plains winter:

When she [Marie] went out into the dark kitchen to fix her plants for the night, she used to stand by a window and look out at the white fields, or watch the currents of snow whirling over the orchard. (OP 202)

And elsewhere:

While Alexandra removed her hat and veil, Mrs. Lee went out to the kitchen and settled herself in a wooden rocking-chair by the stove, looking with great interest at the table, set for three, with a white cloth, and a pot of pink geraniums in the middle. "My, a-an't you gotta fine plants; such-a much flower. How you keep from freeze?"

She pointed to the window shelves, full of blooming fuchsias and geraniums.

"I keep the fire all night, Mrs. Lee, and when it's very cold I put them all on the table, in the middle of the room. Other nights I only put newspapers behind them. Frank laughs at me for fussing, but when they don't bloom he says, 'What's the matter with the darned things?'" (OP 191–92)

The kitchen adjunct most frequently mentioned by Cather is, significantly, that which was perhaps the most important to the pioneers: the cellar.

There were, frequently, icehouses, where ice was stored for the approaching summer after having been cut on a nearby pond or river during the winter. The ice could last well through the summer, until the first frost, when ice no longer was needed to preserve food. (The icehouse often then became the smokehouse for winter slaughtering, only to become the icehouse again in February, when the ice was thick and the smoking season was well past.)

During the winter, meat might simply be hung in the barn and cut as needed, and hams, bacon, and so forth might be buried deep in the oats bin, where mice, dogs, and skunks would not bother it. But more often than not the place for cool storage of all manner of foods, the place to put canned goods so that they would not freeze or be bothered by varmints, was the cellar.

The cellar shelves were the place for canned goods (actually, of course, "jarred" goods), the back floor and raised shoulders were for roots, such as onions, potatoes, and turnips, and strings of onion and garlic might hang from the post supports.

The cellar was not only a haven against famine, it also served on many occasions to save a prairie family from the horrors of tornadoes, prairie fires, hailstorms. I have spent a few evenings myself huddled in a storm cellar, waiting for the world to end above me. It is a curious mixture of remarkable comfort—all the family gathered around amid a wealth of foodstuffs in almost total security—and terror, knowing that everything that was home might be in a state of splintering only feet away.

The cellar was also a place of mixed motives. In some ways, the cellar was the most basic concentration of what a mother and wife was; it represented her dedication and contribution to the survival of the family. On the other hand, it was also the very place where the most profane and secret rituals of the family occurred.

I remember my Aunt Anna taking me to her basement and showing me the arrays of canned goods on her shelves. She explained to me that the jars of pears, beans, beef, beets, pickles, kraut, jelly, jam, and mysteries I don't recall were not arranged according to color or convenience, but according to her personal sense of aesthetics: what it was that looked good. It was also where my Uncle Henry went to smoke his cigars.

The company rose and drank the bride's health in grape-juice punch. Mr. Royce, however, while the guests were being seated, had taken Mr. Wheeler down to the fruit cellar, where the two old friends drank off a glass of well-seasoned Kentucky whiskey, and shook hands. (OO 165)

Such passages remind me of a time I was traveling with a friend, Jay Anderson. We were traveling by night from Newcastle, England, to Oslo, Norway. We had decided that this Norwegian liner would be precisely the place to enjoy a genuine Scandinavian sauna.

By the time we got to the ship's sauna, we found that it was in large part occupied by a crew of Norwegian truckers whose trucks were being moved across the North Sea by this same huge ship. That was all right. They seemed like decent-enough fellows and they were interested in Americans who were hardy (or foolhardy) enough to risk a truckers' sauna. They had cranked the heat up to a temperature that would have done a volcano proud, but we were bearing up fine. Everything seemed to be fraternal indeed.

But another group of truckers—Swedes, as I recall—entered the desert-hot room, and one of them began to pour beer on the red-hot rocks. As instantly as the temperature of the air rose, the Norwegian's tempers rose. "By God," one of the burly blonds growled, "a sauna is where bread is baked and babies are born. It's a clean place, and only a damned fool puts beer on the rocks of a clean place!" Jay and I decided it was time to leave the sauna, as congenial as the company seemed to be.

We suspect that Mr. Royce was much like those irreverents who put beer on the rocks. You can drink whiskey in the cellar, but there would be hell to pay if the temple priestess ever caught you violating the sanctuary.

Two such sanctuaries dominate Cather's novels. Her rich descriptions and careful involvement of the cellars in her plots suggest that she understood the reverence that the women held for their cellars and that she shared that respect:

Claude told Mahailey he was going to the cellar to put up the swinging shelf she had been wanting, so the rats couldn't get at her vegetables.

"Thank you, Mr. Claude. I don't know what does make the rats so bad. The cat catches one most every day, too."

"I guess they come up from the barn. I've got a nice wide board down at the garage for your shelf."

The cellar was cemented, cool and dry, with deep closets for canned fruit and flour and groceries, bins for coal and cobs. . . .

While Claude was planing off the board he meant to suspend from the joists, Mahailey left her work and came down to watch him. She made some pretense of hunting for pickled onions, then seated herself upon a cracker box; close at hand there was a plush "spring-rocker" with one arm gone, but it wouldn't have been her idea of good manners to sit there. Her eyes had a kind of sleepy contentment in them as she followed Claude's motions. She watched him as if he were a baby playing. Her hands lay comfortably in her lap. (OO 19–20)

Little wonder that she was comfortable: this was her realm, and now she was sharing it with someone she loved. In one reality she was indeed watching a baby playing. Her search for onions was only a pretense; pickled onions would be an exotic item to search for, and she elected to search for something so unusual that she knew she could not find it. It was only an excuse that would allow her to be there with Claude.

I cannot discuss Ántonia's (Annie Pavelka's) cellar with any objectivity at all. I have stood in the cool mouth of that very cave on a summer day when the leaves withered on Ántonia's lilacs. I have admired the superior work in the brick vaulted entry, and I have smelled the moist dust on the floor. I love Ántonia so much that standing there, able to touch both walls by spreading my arms, I nonetheless felt as if I were in a cathedral dedicated to a particularly benevolent and graced saint.

Ántonia's cellar is the consummate Nebraska pioneer cellar. Her pride in it is the pride that fed the children of the plains, more a kind of poetry than hoarding. We cannot read the following passage without my heart welling full of memories of the cellars and peasant women and farm children and canned fruits and warm moments of our own lives:

When Anna finished her work and washed her hands, she came and stood behind her mother's chair. "Why don't we show Mr. Burden our new fruit cave?" she asked.

We started off across the yard with the children at our heels. The boys were standing by the windmill, talking about the dog; some of them ran ahead to open the cellar door. When we descended, they all came down after us, and seemed quite as proud of the cave as the girls were.

Ambrosch, the thoughtful-looking one who had directed me down by the plum bushes, called my attention to the stout brick walls and the cement floor. "Yes, it is a good way from the house," he admitted. "But, you see, in winter there are nearly always some of us around to come out and get things."

Anna and Yulka showed me three small barrels; one full of dill pickles, one full of chopped pickles, and one full of pickled watermelon rinds.

"You wouldn't believe, Jim, what it takes to feed them all!" their mother exclaimed. "You ought to see the bread we bake on Wednesdays and Saturdays! It's no wonder their poor papa can't get rich, he has to buy so much sugar for us to preserve with. We have our own wheat ground for flour—but then there's that much less to sell."

Nina and Jan, and a little girl named Lucie, kept shyly pointing out to me the shelves of glass jars. They said nothing, but, glancing at me, traced on the glasses with their finger-tips the outline of the cherries and strawberries and crabapples within, trying by a blissful expression of countenance to give me some idea of their deliciousness.

"Show him the spiced plums, mother. Americans don't have those," said one of the older boys. "Mother uses them to make *kolaches*," he added.

Leo, in a low voice, tossed off some scornful remark in Bohemian. I turned to him. "You think I don't know what *kolaches* are, eh? You're mistaken, young man. I've eaten your mother's *kolaches* long before that Easter Day when you were born." (MA 337–38)

Now we are approaching the message of Cather's foods. We know that a cellar is basically a cold, dank place where one is liable to find rats, spiders, and toads, darkness and cold. But the warmth that the cooks have put into the foods stored there transforms the cellars into temples full of soul-warming spirits. Kitchens are smoky places of heavy and continuous labor. But the pride of the craftsmen who use the tools there makes it the workshop of masters whose jewels may be less permanent than diamonds, but no less valuable.

We have searched in vain for an etymological connection that seems obvious and inevitable, one linking the words *heart, hearth,* and *earth,* but we have found nothing. It is apparently only a linguistic accident, but what a happy accident! We are firmly convinced that the romance that a fireplace has for me is a vestigal remnant of whatever importance the fireside once must have held for the home that huddled only a few feet around it. It was the place of warmth and safety, of food and culture, where the stories were told and the songs were sung.

Cather's kitchens are places of fire and hearth. They are places where the important transactions of life are negotiated. Here Cather abandons subtlety quite purposely; there is after all little sense in being coy about what is by its own nature blunt.

In the isolation and brutality of the plains winter it is not simply home that beckons the traveler, but the kitchen. The kitchen is not just a place where food is prepared; it is a place where souls are rescued and protected:

The basement kitchen seemed heavenly safe and warm in those days—like a tight little boat in a winter sea. (MA 65)

It has always surprised us how a simple kerosene lantern can send out a light that we can see almost a half-mile away from our own log farmhouse near Dannebrog, Nebraska, how that flame no bigger than a thumb can be seen almost a half-hour's walk away. We read Cather and are amazed to find our own feelings put into words we could never find on our own, on such occasions, and it is those resonances that make Cather's writing intoxicatingly personal for us. We read a passage like the following and wonder if perhaps there is not some of Neighbour Rosicky in us—and hope that there is:

> Rosicky shook out his pipe and walked home across the fields. Ahead of him the lamplight shone from his kitchen windows. Suppose he were still in a tailor shop on Vesey Street, with a bunch of pale, narrow-chested sons working on machines, all coming home tired and sullen to eat supper in a kitchen that was a parlour also; with another crowded, angry family quarrelling just across the dumb-waiter shaft, and squeaking pulleys at the windows where dirty washings hung on dirty lines above a court full of old brooms and mops and ash-cans. . . .
>
> He stopped by the windmill to look up at the frosty winter stars and draw a long breath before he went inside. That kitchen with the shining windows was dear to him; but the sleeping fields and bright stars and the noble darkness were dearer still. (NR 93–94)

Cather's kitchens glow of fire. It is only rarely the light of a lamp or lantern; it is the unique dry heat of the stove that glows from her kitchens:

> The sun was gone; the frozen streets stretched long and blue before me; the lights were shining pale in kitchen windows, and I could smell the suppers cooking as I passed. Few people were abroad, and each one of them was hurrying toward a fire. The glowing stoves in the houses were like magnets. (MA 173)

> The little house on the hillside was so much the colour of the night that we could not see it as we came up the draw. The ruddy windows guided us—the light from the kitchen stove, for there was no lamp burning. (MA 52–53)

In summer, activity revolved around the stove because that is where all food was prepared; in winter, life depended on the stove for preserving warmth. It is hard for an outsider to imagine a plains winter. The ground becomes as hard as iron. In the night the trees pop as they split open from the cold. The rivers crack and groan. When the sky is clear, there are more stars than can be imagined. And when there is a blizzard, you can hope to God that you are at home near that stove.

Cather's Ivar has always been a haunting figure for me. I find it unsettling to identify so closely with a character called crazy, but the descriptions of his land, character, and sentiments are so close to my own that it is almost as if Ivar and I were somehow brothers. His comforts are the sort of comforts I appreciate:

In cold weather he sits by the kitchen fire and makes hammocks or mends harness until it is time to go to bed. Then he says his prayers at great length behind the stove, puts on his buffalo-skin coat and goes out to his room in the barn. (OP 87)

Making hammocks, mending harness, or saying prayers, the fire is the lodestone:

On those bitter, starlit nights, as we sat around the old stove that fed us and warmed us and kept us cheerful, we could hear the coyotes howling down by the corrals, and their hungry, wintry cry used to remind the boys of wonderful animal stories; about grey wolves and bears in the Rockies, wildcats and panthers in the Virginia mountains. Sometimes Fuchs could be persuaded to talk about the outlaws and desperate characters he had known. I remember one funny story about himself that made grandmother, who was working her bread on the bread-board, laugh until she wiped her eyes with her bare arm, her hands being floury. (MA 68)

If kitchens abound in Cather's prairie works, it is no surprise that they are peopled with many and varied cooks. The best of the cooks—Mahailey, Mary, and Mary—shine forth best within descriptions of kitchens, meals, and the activities of cooking. Other minor characters are described primarily in terms of their relationships with food and kitchens. Annabelle Chapin, for example,

chanted her lessons over and over to herself while she cooked and scrubbed. . . . Last winter she had recited the odes of Horace about the house . . . until Claude feared he would always associate that poet with the heaviness of hurriedly prepared luncheons (OO 30) and Crazy Ivar knows that insanity is not so much a matter of being dangerous as of being different:

"Look at Peter Kralik. . . . He could work as good as any man, and his head was clear, but they locked him up for being different in his stomach." (OP 93)

The scandalous three Marys of *My Ántonia,* on the other hand, found redemption in their culinary skills for a wide spectrum of sins ranging from giddiness to unsanctioned pregnancy:

The three Marys were considered as dangerous as high explosives to have about the kitchen, yet they were such good cooks and such admirable housekeepers that they never had to look for a place. (MA 203)

In *One of Ours,* Claude Wheeler seems to have his life defined in terms of cooks. From Mrs. Erlich's urban Lincoln kitchen with complex French meals, he returns (OO 41–42) to Mahailey's simple small-town kitchen with one-ingredient dishes. The region he calls home finds expression in the attitudes of a boardinghouse cook and her rough but decent clientele:

Claude went into a restaurant across the street and ordered an oyster stew. The proprietress, a plump little German woman with a frizzed bang, always remembered him from trip to trip. While he was eating his oysters she told him that she had just finished roasting a chicken with sweet po-tatoes, and if he liked he could have the first brown cut off the breast before the train-men came in for dinner. Asking her to bring it along, he waited, sitting on a stool, his boots on the lead-pipe foot-rest, his elbows on the shiny brown counter, staring at a pyramid of tough looking bun-sand-wiches under a glass globe.

"I been lookin' for you every day," said Mrs. Voigt when she brought his plate. "I put plenty good gravy on dem sweet pertaters, ja."

"Thank you. You must be popular with your boarders."

She giggled. "Ja, all de train-men is friends mit me. Sometimes dey bring me a liddle Schweizerkäse from one of dem big saloons in Omaha what de Cherman beobles batronize. I ain't got no boys mein own self, so I got to fix up liddle tings for dem boys, eh?"

She stood nursing her stumpy hands under her apron, watching every mouthful he ate so eagerly that she might have been tasting it herself.

Willa Cather and her brother Roscoe dining out in Cheyenne, Wyoming

The train crew trooped in, shouting to her and asking what there was for dinner, and she ran about like an excited little hen, chuckling and cackling. Claude wondered whether working-men were as nice as that to old women the world over. He didn't believe so. He liked to think that such geniality was common only in what he broadly called "the West." (oo 32–33)

Cather deliberately draws her characters in terms of their attitude toward food and cooking. Mrs. Voigt loves her men—they are all her sons—and her men love her; that is to say, she cooks well for them and they appreciate her food. Claude's wife, Enid, on the other hand, is a vegetarian and sees food as a biological necessity, not as love. Again Cather's subtlety makes her condemnation of Enid all the more crushing. A descriptive passage like the following seems straightforward and perhaps even positive, for cleanliness and efficiency are implicit in the order of Enid's kitchen:

Enid's kitchen, full of the afternoon sun, glittered with new paint, spotless linoleum, and blue-and-white cooking vessels. In the dining-room the cloth was laid, and the table was neatly set for one. Claude opened the icebox, where his supper was arranged for him; a dish of canned salmon with a white sauce; hardboiled eggs, peeled and lying in a nest of lettuce leaves; a bowl of ripe tomatoes, a bit of cold rice pudding; cream and butter. He placed these things on the table, cut some bread, and after carelessly washing his face and hands, sat down to eat in his working shirt. He propped the newspaper against a red glass water pitcher and read the war news while he had his supper. (OO 173)

But Enid's foods are not highly regarded even by her father. When Claude approaches him to announce his intentions in regard to Enid, Mr. Royce pulls no punches, goes directly to the heart of the matter, lays it on the line, discusses his daughter's eating habits:

"Marriage is a final sort of thing, Claude. . . . Enid is a vegetarian, you know. . . ."

Claude smiled. "That could hardly make any difference to me, Mr. Royce."

The other nodded slightly. "I know. At your age you think it doesn't. Such things do make a difference, however." (OO 128)

If Enid's audience does not appreciate her culinary performances, her fellow cooks could be bitingly critical:

"Well, anyhow, I guess Claude had more to eat when Brother Weldon was staying there. Preacher won't be fed on calories, or whatever it is Enid calls 'em," said Susie, who was given to looking on the bright side of things. "Claude's wife keeps a wonderful kitchen; but so could I, if I never cooked any more than she does." (OO 176)

Finally, Cather sums up the situation with Enid in her own words:

[Mr. Miller's hired help] complained of the gloom of the house, and said they could not get enough to eat. Mrs. Royce went every summer to a vegetarian sanatorium in Michigan, where she learned to live on nuts and toasted cereals. She gave her family nourishment, to be sure, but there was never during the day a meal that a man could look forward to with pleasure, or sit down to with satisfaction. (OO 107)

The tactless Mrs. Shimerda seems to take little pride in most parts of her domestic life, but she does insist on her superiority when it comes to food:

> After dinner, when she was helping to wash the dishes, she said, tossing her head: "You got many things for cook. If I got all things like you, I make much better." (MA 89)

It may seem as if we are stretching things a bit, but Crazy Ivar also has strict standards about the quality of his "cooking." Here we are not talking about *his* vegetarianism (OP 43), but about the way he feeds his family, his pigs:

> "You feed them swill and such stuff? Of course! And sour milk? Oh yes! And keep them in a stinking pen? I tell you, sister, the hogs of this country are put upon! . . . Give them only grain and clean feed, such as you would give horses or cattle." (OP 44–45)

Meals at Cather's tables are more social than culinary. Again and again the meals she describes are finished but the diners do not leave the table. Instead they sit and smoke and talk. They talk about the weather (NR 96), news of the day (OO 208), and family business (MA 113). Diners understand that the table is where information is to be distributed and gathered:

> Marie caught Frank's arm and dragged him to the same table, managing to get seats opposite the Bergson's so that she could hear what they were talking about. (OP 218)

The cooks and serving girls are not treated as extraneous elements to meals but are in some cases the very actors who make the meals what they are to be:

> Emil reached home a little past noon, and when he went into the kitchen Alexandra was already seated at the head of the long table, having dinner with her men, as she always did unless there were visitors. He slipped into his empty place at his sister's right. The three pretty young Swedish girls who did Alexandra's housework were cutting pies, refilling coffee-cups, placing platters of bread and meat and potatoes upon the red tablecloth, and continually getting in each other's way between the table and the stove. To be sure they always wasted a good deal of time getting in

each other's way and giggling at each other's mistakes. But, as Alexandra had pointedly told her sisters-in-law, it was to hear them giggle that she kept three young things in her kitchen; the work she could do herself, if it were necessary. (OP 85)

Cather's care for detail is the key to the grand scale of her literary paintings. Alexandra seated at the head of the table, her brother at her right, is a powerful statement about the hierarchy of the family. Cather may speak through male protagonists, but the heads of her tables, the power figures at the table, where it is important to be a power figure, are women:

What a tableful we were at supper: two long rows of restless heads in the lamplight, and so many eyes fastened excitedly upon Ántonia as she sat at the head of the table, filling the plates and starting the dishes on their way. The children were seated according to a system; a little one next an older one, who was to watch over his behaviour and to see that he got his food. Anna and Yulka left their chairs from time to time to bring fresh plates of *kolaches* and pitchers of milk. (MA 347)

If Cather's supper is the social event of the day, her breakfast is the culinary one, and often this is still true today on farms where old ways prevail. Breakfast was seen as the foundation of the day, and niggardliness with visitors was viewed as dismally as it might be with the family. In "Neighbour Rosicky" (309–10), Doctor Burleigh is described as having a particularly deep affection for Mrs. Rosicky (Annie Pavelka, who later was to have the literary name Ántonia). He had been out all night delivering a baby at Tom Marshall's farm, where there was all manner of expensive machinery and stock and feed but no comfort. No comfort for the family, no comfort—or breakfast—for guests. Even if breakfast had been offered, he "refused any breakfast in that slovenly house" and traveled on in his buggy instead to the Rosicky house, where hospitality and meals were warm:

He had driven in just when the boys had come back from the barn and were washing up for breakfast. The long table, covered with a bright oilcloth, was set out with dishes waiting for them, and the warm kitchen was full of the smell of coffee and hot biscuit and sausage. Five big handsome boys, running from twenty to twelve, all with what Burleigh called natural good manners,—they hadn't a bit of the painful self-consciousness he himself had to struggle with when he was a lad. One ran to put his horse away, another helped him off with his fur coat and hung it up, and Josephine, the youngest child and the only daughter, quickly set another place under her mother's direction. . . . "And to think of your being up all night and then not able to get a decent breakfast! I don't know what's the matter with such people."

"Why, Mother," said one of the boys, "if Doctor Ed had got breakfast there, we wouldn't have him here. So you ought to be glad."

"He knows I'm glad to have him, John, any time. But I'm sorry for that poor woman, how bad she'll feel the Doctor had to go away in the cold without his breakfast."

"I wish I'd been in practice when these were getting born." The doctor looked down the row of close-clipped heads. "I missed some good breakfasts by not being."

The boys began to laugh at their mother because she flushed so red, but she stood her ground and threw up her head. "I don't care, you wouldn't have got away from this house without breakfast. No doctor ever did. I'd have had something ready fixed that Anton could warm up for you."

The boys laughed harder than ever, and exclaimed at her: "I'll bet you would!" "She would, that!"

"Father, did you get breakfast for the doctor when we were born?"

"Yes, and he used to bring me my breakfast, too, mighty nice. I was always awful hungry!" Mary admitted with a guilty laugh. (NR 75–78)

It is certainly not by accident that Cather has Rosicky dreaming, as winter comes on, of precisely those kinds of times:

Well, it was a nice snowstorm; a fine sight to see the snow falling so quietly and graciously over so much open country. On his cap and shoulders, on the horses' backs and manes, light, delicate, mysterious it fell; and with it a dry cool fragrance was released into the air. It meant rest for vegetation and men and beasts, for the ground itself; a season of long nights for sleep, leisurely breakfasts, peace by the fire. (NR 81)

It is not by accident that Claude Wheeler's last meal in his Nebraska home, before he leaves for the wars of Europe, is a breakfast, Mahailey still fretting about her photograph of the dislocated women who lost their stoves and dishes. (OO 223–24) Mahailey's concern is Claude's too, and in concert with Claude's understanding of what good life was about:

To be assured, at his age, of three meals a day and plenty of sleep, was like being assured of a decent burial. (OO 89)

Meals, of course, are more than day-to-day activities, whether they are viewed as social events or merely as times to feed the body. There are also those occasions when food becomes ritual or celebration, and Cather, with her care, was not likely to miss those observations. In a passage cited earlier it was noted that when a traveling evangelist visited, or the village minister, it was a time for special food, something more than mere calories, or whatever it was that Enid called them:

The confirmation service followed the Mass. When it was over, the congregation thronged about the newly confirmed. The girls, and even the boys, were kissed and embraced and wept over. All the aunts and grandmothers wept with joy. The housewives had much ado to tear themselves away from the general rejoicing and hurry back to their kitchens. The country parishioners were staying in town for dinner, and nearly every house in Sainte-Agnes entertained visitors that day. Father Duchesne, the bishop, and the visiting priests dined with Fabien Sauvage, the banker. (OP 256)

Plains pioneer accounts are redolent with narratives about the visit of the minister. Rarely did anyone more important than the minister come to visit, and when he did the dinner table groaned as it did otherwise only on the occasion of threshing:

Claude's mother was not discriminating about preachers. She believed them all chosen and sanctified and was never happier than when she had one in the house to cook for and wait upon. She made Mr. Weldon [the preacher] so comfortable that he remained under her roof for several weeks, occupying the spare room, where he spent the mornings in study and meditation. He appeared regularly at mealtime to ask a blessing upon the food and to sit with devout, downcast eyes while the chicken was being dismembered. . . . His meekness amused Mr. Wheeler, who liked to ply him with food and never failed to ask him gravely "what part of the chicken he would prefer," in order to hear him murmur, "A little of the white meat, if you please." (OO 28)

Nothing is quite so rude as explaining a joke. It suggests that the audience is too dense to understand, but the fact of the matter is, if they don't they never will; if they do, the conclusion must be that the explainer was too dense to understand that. But is it clear to the reader that in this passage Mr. Wheeler is confronting the unctuous, parasitic minister with the threat of his having to say aloud, at the table, *breast*.

Cather shows us Mrs. Royce's coldness by telling us that her meals "gave her family nourishment . . . but there was never during the day a meal that a man could look forward to with pleasure, or sit down to with satisfaction" (OO 107), and the parallel is continued in that although she is famous for the mayonnaise and angel food cake she makes for public show at the church dinners, her husband must retreat to the hotel dining room for a meal he can truly enjoy. (OO 107)

That festival is part of the meal is never a doubt in Cather's works. And there is a marvelous range in the festival, from the dramatically elegant to the wonderfully simple. The acme of the elegant is Jim Burden's observance of a theatrical production of a meal in a play in Lincoln:

This introduced the most brilliant, worldly, the most enchantingly gay scene I had ever looked upon. I had never seen champagne bottles opened on the stage before—indeed, I had never seen them opened anywhere. The memory of that supper makes me hungry now; the sight of it then, when I had only a students' boarding-house dinner behind me, was delicate torment. (MA 273)

Other festival meals range from school picnics (MA 340), church dinners (OP 212), and wedding suppers (OP 227) to the wonderful simplicity and serenity of a country picnic for two:

There were days, too, which she and Emil had spent together, upon which she loved to look back. There had been such a day when they were down on the river in the dry year, looking over the land. They had made an early start one morning and had driven a long way before noon. When Emil said he was hungry, they drew back from the road, gave Brigham his oats among the bushes, and climbed up to the top of a grassy bluff to eat their lunch under the shade of some little elm trees. The river was clear there, and shallow, since there had been no rain, and it ran in ripples over the sparkling sand. Under the hanging willows of the opposite bank there was an inlet where the water was deeper and flowed so slowly that it seemed to sleep in the sun. In this little bay a single duck was swimming and diving and preening her feathers, disporting herself very happily in the flickering light and shade. They sat for a long time, watching the solitary bird take its pleasure. . . . Alexandra remembered that day as one of the happiest in her life (OP 204–5)

There is a picnic in the short story "Neighbour Rosicky" that has always struck me as being a particularly warm circumstance. Rosicky returns from the fields on a hot Fourth of July and finds his wife, Mary, making plum preserves. He orders up a special supper for the holiday and kills a couple of chickens.

In the meantime, Rosicky takes three hot children and all of them go for a splash in the horse tank. Now that is all well and good, but who should drive up that moment for a visit but the preacher! Rosicky covers himself with one of his children and carries on the conversation from the horse tank.

The family packs up the food and goes to a grove of linden trees near some mulberries and has a Fourth of July picnic:

"So we carried our supper down, an' a bottle of my wild-grape wine, an' everything tasted good, I can tell you. The wind got cooler as the sun was goin' down, and it turned out pleasant, only I noticed how the leaves was curled up on the linden trees. That made me think, an' I asked your father if that hot wind all day hadn't been terrible hard on the gardens an' the corn.

"'Corn,' he says, 'there ain't no corn.'

"'What you talkin' about?' I said. 'Ain't we got forty acres?'

"'We ain't got an ear,' he says, 'nor nobody else ain't got none. All the corn in this country was cooked by three o'clock today, like you'd roasted it in an oven.'

"'You mean you won't get no crop at all?' I asked him. I couldn't believe it, after he'd worked so hard.

Willa Cather at a picnic at the old golf course, Red Cloud, Nebraska

" 'No crop this year,' he says, 'That's why we're havin' a picnic. We might as well enjoy what we got.' " (NR 98)

One of the problems in writing about Cather and her treatment and use of food is that her message is so clear and so frequently stated. There is an interesting and substantial difference between redundancy and repetition. Powerful music and powerful literature use the same word or phrase or idea over and over and over again without the word, phrase, or idea becoming worn in the repetition. It actually gathers strength. Cather does that.

Again and again she tells us that food equals love, and the result is not at all that we become tired of the idea or suspicious of it; instead, we become convinced of it. I suspect this is in part because we know that what she is saying is true because we have thought it too but never have thought it in words quite so well crafted. What we eat has little to do with what tastes good or what is cheap or what is available or what is good for us; we eat what we eat because it means something to us. For Cather it means love:

With Mary, to feed creatures was the natural expression of affection,—her chickens, the calves, her big hungry boys. It was a rare pleasure to feed a young man whom she seldom saw and of whom she was as proud as if he belonged to her. (NR 76)

Mahailey, moving about the stove, watched over the group at the table. She liked to see the men fill themselves with food. . . . (OO 83)

There was a basic harmony between Ántonia and her mistress. They had strong, independent natures, both of them. . . . They liked to prepare rich, hearty food and to see people eat it. . . . (MA 180)

[Mrs. Erlich] took him into the kitchen and explained the almost holy traditions that governed this complicated cookery. Her excitement and seriousness as she beat and stirred were very pretty, Claude thought. She told off on her fingers the many ingredients, but he believed there were things she did not name: the fragrance of old friendships, the glow of early memories, her belief in wonder-working rhymes and songs. Surely these were fine things to put into little cakes! (OO 41)

Cather uses the words *food* and *comfort* in the same breath, almost synonymously (MA 98), and the primal gift is to feed the one you love:

". . . I want to cook your supper myself." (MA 344)

"Let's get up a nice supper, and not let your mother help at all; make her be company for once." (NR 102)

The significance of the gift was not lost on the recipients. In a scene that explains so much of what America is really about, Rosicky tells his children about his youth, when he starved and slaved in the gutters of the Old World. He explains to them what famine means and the lengths to which a hungry boy will go to survive, telling them his own experiences as a starving migrant in England. His children cry, "Poor little Papa, I don't want him to be hungry!" and he tells them in one sentence what their family and migration to America mean:

"Da's long ago, child. I ain't never been hungry since I had your mudder to cook fur me." (NR 100)

Enid, on the other hand, the wife who eventually deserts her husband, Claude, serves him a cold and proper meal, prepared for good nourishment rather than love, and leaves him to eat it alone. (OO 173) The import is not at all subtle.

That food is essential to an understanding of Cather can be seen not only in the fact that she uses food as a motif determining character, geography, ethnicity, and historical context, but also in her use of food so extensively as a descriptive metaphor. I would like to argue not that she uses food more than classical allusion or music but that the food metaphor is there and that its importance cannot be denied:

His head was the shape of a chocolate drop. (MA 285–86)
My nose looked like a big blue plum. (MA 249)
The air was clear and heady as wine. (MA 43)
His pale face was as bare as an egg. (OP 55)
"My garden all cut to pieces like sauerkraut." (OP 60)

Everywhere the grain stood ripe and the hot afternoon was full of the smell of the ripe wheat, like the smell of bread baking in the oven. (OP 257–58)

The brown iris [of her eyes] . . . was curiously slashed with yellow, the color of sunflower honey. (OP 135)

"And look at them Fassler children! Pale, pinched little things, they look like skimmed milk." (NR 84)

[Peter was] bow-legged, and fat as butter. (MA 34)

His . . . face . . . was like a melon among its leaves. (MA 34)

And not even the most common of Cather's metaphors, the red of the prairie grasses, is totally separate from her constant preoccupation with food:

Presently, against one of those banks, I saw a sort of shed, thatched with the same wine-coloured grass that grew everywhere. (MA 22)

Foods

The recipes in the following chapters dealing with Willa Cather's works are drawn from a variety of sources. Our intent has been to use recipes as close to Cather as possible, so that you might be able to reproduce the foods she was thinking about as she wrote. We are not asserting that these foods are indeed authentic pioneer Nebraska foods, only that they were close enough to Cather herself that they were her idea of what the dishes are.

As I suggest elsewhere in these pages, the best traditional recipes are not written down. Someone simply knows how to make the food. A little of this, some of that, enough of those, and there it is. Moreover, many parts of the world—parts where Cather's migrant characters came from—do not see recipes as we do, as rigid formulas that are to be followed as precisely as possible for guaranteed success. European cookbooks often list ingredients but leave the proportions up to the cook. That is the skill *you* are supposed to bring to the kitchen.

The bulk of the recipes reproduced here come from the Cather kitchens. The Willa Cather Pioneer Memorial has a large file of the family's cookbooks and recipes, and with the help of Ann Billesbach we copied the relevant ones and reproduce them here. Some are from the three cookbooks in the collection: *The Home Queen Cook Book* (Chicago: M. A. Donohue and Company, 1893; Fort Dearborn Publishing, 1900; H. Chandler, 1901; and M. A. Donohue, 1901); *The White House Cook Book* by Hugo Zieman and Mrs.

G. L. Gillette (New York, Akron, Chicago: Saalfield Publishing Company, 1887; F. L. Gillette, 1894; Weiner Company, 1899; Weiner Company, 1905); and *Domestic Cookery* by Elizabeth Ellicott Lea (Baltimore: Cushings and Bailey, 1853).

If wear, tear, and stains can be used as an index of usage, the favorite cookbook of the Cather kitchen library was Mrs. Lea's *Domestic Cookery.* The first several pages are missing, recipes have been pasted on the endpapers, pages are dog-eared, marked, and punctured with straight pins. The book measures 7½ by 4½ inches and contains 310 pages. In addition to food recipes it contains a guide for young wives; dyeing information; recipes for poultices and ointments; directions for making feather beds (and a loose clipping on the same subject); sections on bathing and cleaning knives, forks, and teeth; cultivation of flowers; and "hints on the management of domestics." It is impossible to know which edition the Cather copy represents, but it is identical to the 1853 edition reproduced by William Woys Weaver and discussed in detail below.

The *Home Queen* measures 9½ by 7 inches and contains 608 pages, but some pages may be missing from the end of the Cather copy. It has been well used and marked, but only a fraction of that of the Lea cookbook. The Cather copy has many inserts, including one for using Puritan oil cookstoves. Indeed, the book seems to have been used as a file box. There are sections on sample menus, napkin folding, table settings, and carving.

The *White House Cook Book* measures 7 by 9¾ inches and contains 590 pages. It has menus (including one for a state dinner at the White House), formal arrangements, medicinal formulas, cleaning compounds, and etiquette. The Cather copy has been used, but much less than Mrs. Lea's book and even the *Home Queen*; it is clean and rarely marked. The book's recipes are mostly contributions from two hundred respondents, "among whom are the wives of the Governors and Congressmen, and many other ladies equally well qualified to contribute to our book. Every State and Territory is represented." Although the title, *The White House Cook Book,* suggests haute cuisine, the content and appeal is that of domestic mass culture, a conclusion which is demonstrated by the appearance of

The White House Cook Book at auctions and on Goodwill shelves throughout America today.

A remarkable and happy coincidence is the publication a few years ago of William Woys Weaver's book *A Quaker Woman's Cookbook: The Domestic Cookery of Elizabeth Ellicott Lea* (University of Pennsylvania Press: Philadelphia, 1982). Weaver stresses the contention that I have made above: although the Cathers used cookbooks in their kitchens, the substance of their daily fare was traditional folk foodways. He writes, "What is remarkable about Elizabeth Lea's cookbook is that a Quaker widow in Maryland has compiled a collection of recipes that forms one of the most varied samplings of the rural American folk cookery of her era." (p. xv)

As a folklorist, I might have been disappointed to find that so much of Willa Cather's food experience was elitist, taken from cookbooks representing a cultural level quite apart from the frontier homes she described in her novels. As we worked through the Cather recipe files, however, we were struck by the homely inventories offered in the three volumes of the Cather cookbook library and by the even more humble choices that were identified in those books by commentary, marks, or markers.

Weaver underscores our own conclusions: "While this [personal quality] may have detracted from the social merits of Elizabeth Lea's book in the eyes of Quaker intellectuals, it did add an aspect to her work which is not found in many other American cookbooks of the period: that is, a noticeable 'folk' perception in the selection and composition of her recipes. For her cookery, if anything, was matter-of-fact in its simplicity not over-intellectualized or studied. Her cookery was traditional. Her folk recipes were in some cases outright poverty food." (p. xxviii)

Had the Cather family enjoyed an elegant, high-style Victorian menu, it would not have detracted from Willa's remarkable skill in capturing the look, taste, smell, and feel of the plains rural kitchen. It is a comfort for the folklorist, on the other hand, to find that the reason Cather understood the peasant table so well is because she grew up at one.

Just as we have recommended that this book be read with

Cather's writings at hand, we also recommend Weaver's reproduction of *Domestic Cookery* as a remarkable opportunity to add to one's own cookbook selection the single most important cookbook in Willa Cather's Red Cloud childhood, providing a rare historical context for this study.

We sought in these printed works especially the recipes that are circled, starred, underlined, or marked, perhaps with a bent page corner. Other recipes are from period magazines and newspapers but had been cut out and inserted in the pages of the cookbooks, glued to the end boards, or even attached to the pages with straight pins. The real prizes were the recipes hastily scribbled on spelling forms, bank slips, or used envelopes. Many of them were so tattered with age, stained and spotted by kitchen disasters that they could hardly be read, but what better testimony could we hope for to prove *this* recipe's popularity in the Cather family?

Next we solicited recipes from friends, neighbors, and members of the Cather family, hoping that a lentil soup recipe from Red Cloud might be closer to Cather's lentil soup than a Minneapolis version. Finally we turned to our own German and Czech families, assuming that a *kolache* filling recipe from a Czech aunt is closer to the mark than an "official" recipe from another book.

In the case of all of the recipes from the Cather file and from her relatives, friends, and neighbors, and from our files and those of our relatives and friends, it must be kept in mind that they are usually hastily written notes jotted down to jar the cook's own memory. That is, recipes from home files are not usually meant for others to read. They may be in a kind of shorthand that the cook understands but which is very confusing to us. Frankly, that is the charm of these recipes. It may be frustrating not to have precise directions or to find words that we simply cannot interpret, and yet it is these very confusions that demonstrate that we have penetrated to the heart of Cather's kitchens.

Willa Cather was too skilled and careful a writer to leave important literary matters to chance. When she said "corn meal mush," she meant a particular kind of corn meal mush. But in the end we can only hope to come close to whatever particular flavor she was thinking of. We hope that we have been faithful to Cather, the Great Plains and our readers with our searches and selections. I frequently argue within the University of Nebraska–Lincoln English Department that our graduate students cannot know plains literature if they do not know the plains. To a degree that same thing may be true for central motifs in Cather's works, including foodways. Surely we understand her words about the taste of a white mulberry better if we have tasted a white mulberry. Ántonia's kitchen comes alive for us if we know the smell of baking *kolaches,* and *only* if we know the smell of baking *kolaches*.

Food is peculiar stuff. We have adjectives to describe sights and sounds, but not many that convey tastes and smells to us in such a way that we can reproduce them in our minds. How do you describe the smell of Benedictine to someone who has never known its perfume? How does one tell a lifelong vegetarian about the taste of a rare tenderloin? It doesn't, after all, taste like anything but rare tenderloin.

To that degree, then, let this book help you reproduce and enjoy some of the tastes and smells of Cather's kitchens.

The recipes presented here are reproduced as they appear in the Cather family files, in the cookbooks from the Cather kitchen, and from the files of contributors who helped us with recipes we could not find within the Cather archives. Obviously, many of the recipes antedate modern cooking techniques and theories and anyone attempting to reproduce these foods should use whatever skills, knowledge, tools, and techniques are currently available to make food better and safer. Especially in processes like canning, all care should be taken to make these early recipes as safe as modern techniques can make them.

Many of the recipes we found are incomplete, unclear, confusing, or illegible. The only guarantee the authors or publishers can offer for the recipes is the assurance of our best wishes. Consider them to be suggestions rather than directions, archaeological remnants rather than blueprints, mysteries rather than maps.

Meat

During the early years of settlement and travel, big game—buffalo, elk, antelope, and deer—frequently was downed and roasted over an open fire. What was not eaten was left to rot. As I have mentioned, the settlers avoided using the very efficient Indian methods of preservation—drying, for example—because of problems with status.

Big game was quickly eradicated on the plains, or at least reduced to the point where it could no longer be consider a principal food source. The homesteader still needed meat but could only rarely afford to butcher his precious stock for himself and his family. It was at that point that the lowly rabbit assumed a significance far above his modest station in life. Young boys and girls on their way to bring the cows in for milking carried the family's .22-caliber rifle in the hope of bringing home the meat as well as the milk. It is not surprising, then, that recipes for rabbit abound in pioneer records.

I grew up on the plains and I understood a meal to mean meat. For me, a Lutheran, there were meatless meals like Good Friday, when we ate only *Schnitzsupp* (dried fruit soup) and *Grebel* (doughnuts), and for my wife, Linda, a Nebraska-born and raised Catholic, there were Fridays, Holy Days, and Christmas Eve, when the meat was fish, but those were exceptions to the rule: meat is the entree to our meals. To that degree (and many others) we are products of our German and Czech lower-middle-class plains upbringing.

Cather's pioneers were meat eaters too. As we have pointed out in early chapters, meat was abundant on the frontier because it ran wild at every hand. But Cather's characters are not on the frontier in its rawest sense. (I should make it clear here however that we believe that plainsmen are still on the frontier today: we are still struggling to understand this landscape and to deal with it. But we are no longer settling it. Actually, we are now retreating from it. Every year the population of the countryside of the Great Plains, that part of it which is most distinctive, is ever more sparse.)

By the time Cather's people were struggling with the plains

Fourth Avenue Market, Red Cloud, Nebraska, 1922. Left to right:
Harry Yost, John E. Yost (owner), Charles Eggleston, an employee,
Jake Ellinger (man seen in mirror)

there were such things as butcher shops (MA 196). In the cities, like
Lincoln with its considerable sophistication for the time, in com-
parison with towns like Red Cloud, food could be quite elegant.
Claude Wheeler could visit Mrs. Erlich's home and enjoy a Conti-
nental meal:

If Mrs. Erlich and her Hungarian woman made lentil soup and potato
dumplings and Wiener-Schnitzel for him, it only made the plain fare on the
farm seem the heavier. (OO 73)

The following recipe for roast veal and lamb is the closest we
could find to Wienerschnitzel in the Cather papers; it comes from
Mrs. Lea's *Domestic Cookery*:

Veal should be well seasoned, and rubbed with lard; when it begins to
brown, baste it with salt and water; a large loin will take from two to three
hours to roast, the thin part of the fore-quarter an hour; it should be well
done; boil up and thicken the gravy. A leg of veal or mutton may be stuffed
before baking.

Lamb and mutton do not require to be rubbed with lard, as they are generally fatter than veal; make the gravy as for veal. A quarter of lamb will roast in an hour; a loin of mutton in two hours. (p. 14)

The kitchen was no longer dependent on the ingenuity of the cook or the generosity of the preceding harvest:

I was glad, when I came home from school at noon, to see a farm-wagon standing in the back yard, and I was always ready to run downtown to get beefsteak or baker's bread for unexpected company. (MA 146)

There are no steak recipes in the Cather files. Fire-grilled steak is a relatively new idea for the kitchen, dependent in large part on the recent availability of fat-marbled meat that can suffer dry cooking. Steaks from grass-fed animals were usually cooked in a gravy. A much more common way of preparing beefsteak was as roast, in the style of this typical recipe from our own recipe file:

Best to make ahead of time. Put meat in roaster on elevated grate. Salt, pepper, and season. Add a little water. Leave uncovered 350° for 30 minutes. Then 300° for 2 hours, depending on size. Turn roast halfway through, salt, pepper, season, and cover for the remaining time. When done, let cool. Slice meat and skim off fat from juice. Before serving: Gravy—make flour paste in cup to get lumps out, put in cold roaster, heat and add potato water (no milk!). For smoother gravy, keep stirring. Add some diluted cornstarch. Put sliced meat in gravy and heat on top of stove.

From the Cathers' *White House Cook Book* (p. 117):

COLD ROAST, WARMED, NO. 1
Cut from the remains of a cold roast the lean meat from the bones into small, thin slices. Put over the fire a frying pan containing a spoonful of butter or drippings. Cut up a quarter of an onion and fry it brown, then remove the onion, add the meat gravy left from the day before, and if not thick enough add a little flour; salt and pepper. Turn the pieces of meat into this and let them simmer a few minutes. Serve hot.

COLD ROAST, WARMED, NO. 2
Cold rare roast beef may be made as good as when freshly cooked by slicing, seasoning with salt, pepper and bits of butter; put it in a plate or pan with a spoonful or two of water, covering closely, and set in the oven until

hot, but no longer. Cold steak may be shaved very fine with a knife and used the same way.

Or, if the meat is in small pieces, cover them with buttered letter paper, twist each end tightly, and boil them on the gridiron, sprinkling them with finely chopped herbs.

Still another way of using cold meats is to mince the lean portions very fine and add to a batter made of one pint of milk, one cup of flour and three eggs. Fry like fritters and serve with drawn butter or sauce.

HAMBURGER STEAK [P. 118]

Take a pound of raw flank or round steak, without any fat, bone or stringy pieces. Chop it until a perfect mince; it cannot be chopped too fine. Also chop a small onion quite fine and mix well with the meat. Season with salt and pepper; make into cakes as large as a biscuit, but quite flat, or into one large flat cake a little less than half an inch thick. Have ready a frying pan with butter and lard mixed; when boiling hot put in the steak and fry brown. Garnish with celery top around the edge of the platter and two or three slices of lemon on the top of the meat.

A brown gravy made from the grease the steak was fried in and poured over the meat enriches it.

From Mrs. Lea's *Domestic Cookery* (p. 14):

Season the beef with pepper and salt and put it in the tin kitchen, well skewered to the spit, with a pint of water in the bottom; baste and turn it frequently, so that every part may have the fire. A very large piece of beef will take three hours to roast; when it is done, pour the gravy out into a skillet, let it boil, and thicken it with flour mixed with water; if it be too fat, skim off the top which will be useful for other purposes.

The character of Claude's father was defined in part by his lack of understanding of the importance of care and planning when it comes to food. But Claude's mother was equipped to deal with the problems. Imagine for the moment what it means suddenly to have to deal with a whole beef. The task of butchering is enough of a problem when it is done according to plan, yet as a spur-of-the-moment crisis. . . .

If he felt like eating roast beef and went out and killed a steer, she did the best she could to take care of the meat, and if some of it spoiled she tried not to worry. (oo 61)

A recipe for beef loaf marked in the Cather copy of *The Home Queen Cook Book* (p. 152):

Take 3½ pounds of beef chopped very fine; round steak is best, 2 well beaten eggs, 6 small crackers rolled fine, 1 cup sweet milk, a piece of butter size of an egg, salt, pepper and sage to taste. Mix well, press into a bread tin, cover with a tin and bake 2½ hours, occasionally basting with butter and hot water.

When beef was butchered the hide was of course saved for all manner of harness repairs, for shoes, gloves, or door hinges. Blood was saved for sausage, bones were boiled down in soup, and even tallow would be saved for candles or soap (MA 81). This was especially true in early pioneer years when kerosene was not yet available for lanterns, and of course bees, which were not native to the continent—much less the plains—had not become common enough to provide wax for candles.

Mahailey, the consummate cook of Cather's writing, thinks constantly in terms of food, and we get a hint of why in a passage from *One of Ours* that alludes to her early life, before we see her and before she came to Claude Wheeler's home; there can be little doubt that Mahailey is in reality Marjorie Anderson, who served as a domestic in Cather's own home in Red Cloud:

Mahailey had had a hard life in her young days, married to a savage mountaineer who often abused her and never provided for her. She could remember times when she sat in the cabin, beside an empty meat-barrel and a cold iron pot, waiting for "him" to bring home a squirrel he had shot or a chicken he had stolen. (OO 21)

In those few lines Cather makes some interesting observations about early life on the frontier. There was, for example, a meat barrel, where meat could be salted and stored. And the cooking was to be done in an iron pot. (If you have never used one, buy one at once; you will never regret it. The even heat and easy cleaning are the practical aspects, but there is also something mighty comforting about a black iron pot simmering, even if it is on a sterile gas stove rather than a cookstove that is a member of the family!)

Mahailey's man was a small figure indeed to steal chickens.

One of the stories we love from Dannebrog, where we have our farm, is of the fellow who did the whole town a favor a few decades ago. When times were tough and chicken feed was scarce, he helped everyone out. He stole their chickens!

More about poultry later, but for the moment let's deal with the "game" at hand: squirrel.

We have encountered quite a few people who will not eat "tree rat," and I will never forget the scolding I took from my daughter Joyce when I first served squirrel. She summarized her objections quite well: she said the problem with eating small animals like squirrels is seeing the whole creature in one piece. We have since dismembered our squirrels or cooked them until the meat fell from the bone.

On the other hand, it was an old friend, Russell Meints, who first called our attention to squirrel and its value. "Finest game you'll ever eat," he said. And he was right. We were astonished. Our farm was overrun by squirrels and they were reduced to eating tree bark every spring by March. So I trimmed the population by hunting them. And we hated to see the meat go to waste so we tried them. Squirrel stew is wonderful. It is one of the mildest, nicest game meats you'll ever try. From Linda's recipe files:

Cut up thoroughly cleaned squirrel [not as easy as it sounds]. Salt, pepper, and roll in flour. Fry in hot lard until brown.

Meanwhile cook potatoes and carrots in boiling water for 10 to 15 minutes.

Remove meat from bones, To pan drippings add flour and potato water. I like to add tomato sauce too and a little poultry seasoning. You can make this stew with any combination of vegetables—peas, onions, etc.

Add meat, after stew thickens and then the potatoes and carrots. Let simmer one hour or until done.

The Cather family files do not include a recipe for squirrel, but the following sample from Alice Styskal of Omaha is representative:

Cut a thoroughly cleaned squirrel into serving pieces. Dip into flour to which you add a little salt and pepper. Fry until nice and brown. Slice an onion over the squirrel. Cover and bake slowly until done.

Anyone who has sampled and enjoyed a succulent quail or experienced the explosion they present as they burst from a patch of wild roses, will understand Claude Wheeler's statement in *One of Ours* (p. 155) that "when a bunch of quail rise out of a cornfield they're a mighty tempting sight, if a man likes hunting."

I am still troubled by people who hunt purely for the pleasure of killing, and yet there is a code among many hunters that comes close to what I admire most about the Plains Indians. They understand the creatures they are killing and that they are—no doubt about it—killing. I am bothered by those hunters who make self-serving statements about hunting to preserve the balance of nature or because they love the outdoors, but I am troubled most by those who eat and do not understand that the very nature of living rests upon the sacrifice of creatures to nourish us. Vegetarianism like Enid's in *One of Ours* is but one variety, that which maintains that vegetarianism is more healthful, a relatively harmless belief in the face of millennia and the reality that we humans are omnivorous. When we eat, things die to nourish us. To deny this serves only to conceal from ourselves the reality of the sacrifice others make for us.

That certainly was no problem on the pioneer plains. People had little time to waste, little money to spare for sport hunting. The pioneer hunted to live. And just as surely as the creatures of God's earth nourished the hunter, he also understood that his body would nourish the soil, which would in turn nourish the wild creatures for another generation to eat. Rural people still understand that inevitable course of events. And Cather, whatever her eventual urban sophistication and whatever the majority preponderance of her literary historians might think today, understood that too. Hunting is a part of her works.

It is not possible to know from the passage what the men are going to hunt on the Niobrara (MA 368–69), but I suspect it is deer or elk. Today the Niobrara is most popular for its turkeys, a population that has been enhanced by the stocking and protection of that magnificent bird.

Most of the turkeys that graced Cather's tables were probably domesticated birds, but sometimes that is not easy to determine. Wild turkeys are perfectly content to join their tamer brothers at the poultry feeder. Turkeys are astonishingly smart, and at the same time remarkably stupid. Any hunter will tell you how wily they can be, and any farmer or rancher will complain how troublesome it is to have hundreds of wild turkeys stealing food from domesticated poultry. Most references in Cather's works are simply to turkey:

He went to shave and change his shirt while the turkey was roasting. Rudolph and Polly were coming over for supper. (NR 96)

A modest passage in *One of Ours* has always struck me as being Cather's statement about how one regards what is presented on the table for a meal:

. . . they all descended to the kitchen to greet the turkey. (OO 79)

The main dish is not simply accepted or acknowledged; the turkey is *greeted*. We are told in the same passage of *One of Ours* that the stuffing for that bird is oyster stuffing. From the Cather's *Home Queen Cook Book* (p. 143), and this may be the very recipe Cather had in mind when she wrote that paragraph:

One quart oysters. Drain liquor off and heat boiling hot. Drop oysters in for 1 minute, skim out, and set the liquor on stove to keep it hot. Cut the oysters into halves. Heat 1 pt. cream or rick [*sic*; rich?] milk, let come to a boil. Cream 1 table-spoon butter and 1 of flour, add to milk. When thick add salt and white pepper; then add liquor boiling hot. Just before taking up, add the oysters. Very nice to serve with turkey.

From an undated and untitled newspaper clipping inserted in the Cather family copy of *The Home Queen Cook Book*:

For a very simple stuffing, shell and blanch a couple of quarts of chestnuts and boil for half an hour in water enough to cover. Drain and mash, adding to them three tablespoonfuls of butter, a level tablespoonful of salt, a saltspoonfull of pepper, a teaspoonful of minced onion, two tablespoons of bread crumbs and the yolks of two eggs. Mix thoroughly and stuff the turkey.

And from the Czech kitchen of Sally Hotovy of Lincoln:

2 loaves bread (cut in small cubes)
3¾ teas. salt
1⅛ teas. pepper
2½ teas. sage
1¼ teas. thyme
5 teas. poultry seasoning
½ cup parsley flakes
1¼ cups shortening
1¼ cups minced onion
½ cup margarine
2½ cups water

Combine bread with salt, pepper, sage, thyme, poultry seasoning, & parsley. Mix thoroughly.

Melt shortening in large container or skillet. Add onion, saute for 2 minutes. Add bread mixture and saute until lightly browned, stirring constantly.

Melt butter in boiling water, pour over browned bread mixture, tossing lightly.

Stuff into cavities of 18–20 lb. turkey, roast.

For turkey gravy add 3 to 4 tablespoons flour to turkey drippings. If making mashed potatoes some potato water may be added to make more gravy. Also some corn starch can be used instead of all flour. Gravy will be smoother.

A substantial number of Cather's references to wild game are specifically to duck. That's not surprising; Czech culture dominates her books and her kitchens, and duck is a mainstay of Czech cuisine. When Lou and Alexandra of *O Pioneers!* are traveling to visit Crazy Ivar, who forbids hunting on his place, they see wild ducks (OP 34–35) and wish they had brought a gun, but of course they could never violate Ivar's trust in that way. (Louis does however sniff, "I'd rather have ducks for supper than Crazy Ivar's tongue.")

Duck is understood to be a special entree for festival dinners like Christmas Day (OP 52) and as special Sunday noon fare with dumplings and homemade sauerkraut, and hunting was and to some extent still is the method for obtaining the dark-meated birds:

There was a sharp crack from the gun, and five of the birds fell to the ground. Emil and his companion laughed delightedly, and Emil ran to pick them up. When he came back, dangling the ducks by their feet, Marie held her apron and he dropped them into it. (OP 127)

From Linda's family recipe file:

Roast duck according to size in moderate oven. Toward end, drain off grease and add water. This makes juice to ladle over the knedlicky (dumplings) and sauerkraut.

From *The White House Cook Book* (pp. 92–93):

Pick, draw, clean thoroughly, and wipe dry. Cut the neck close to the back, beat the breast-bone flat with a rolling pin, tie the wings and legs securely, and stuff with the following:

three pints bread crumbs, six ounces butter, or part butter and salt pork, two chopped onions, and one teaspoonful each of sage, black pepper and salt. Do not stuff very full, and sew up the openings firmly to keep the flavor in and the fat out. If not fat enough, it should be larded with salt pork, or tie a slice upon the breast. Place in a baking pan, with a little water, and baste frequently with salt and water—some add onion, and some vinegar; turn often, so that the sides and back may all be nicely browned. When nearly done, baste with butter and a little flour. These directions will apply to tame geese as well as ducks. Young ducks should roast from twenty-five to thirty minutes, and full-grown ones for an hour or more, with frequent basting. Some prefer them underdone and served very hot; but, as a rule, thorough cooking will prove more palatable. Make a gravy out of the necks and gizzards by putting them in a quart of cold wter, that must be reduced to a pint by boiling. The giblets, when done, may be chopped fine and added to the juice. The preferred seasonings are one tablespoonful of Madeira or sherry, a blade of mace, one small onion, and a little cayenne pepper; strain through a hair seive; pour a little over the ducks and serve the remainder in a boat. Served with jellies or any tart sauce.

One of the most commonly mentioned game meats in Cather's pioneer works is rabbit. Rabbits could be hunted with small-caliber firearms (MA 41), and during times when money was scarce for such things as ammunition they could be caught in traps (OP 61). Rabbits were hunted not only for meat but also for their fine fur:

"My *tatinek* make me little hat with the skins, little hat for winter! . . . Meat for eat, skin for hat." (MA 41)

And children, including Ántonia, did indeed wear caps made of the warm, soft fur:

Ántonia and Yulka came running out, wearing little rabbit-skin hats their father had made for them. (MA 63)

Shimerda's rabbit-skin hat is seen by some as an overt sign of poverty, perhaps Old Worldliness. Fuchs tells Jim Burden,

"He's making himself a rabbit-skin cap, Jim, and a rabbit-skin collar that he buttons on outside his coat. They ain't got but one overcoat among 'em over there, and they take turns wearing it." (MA 70)

One of the most mouth-watering food references in Cather's works deals with rabbit:

They did not eat much, although they had been working in the cold all day, and there was a rabbit stewed in gravy for supper, and prune pies." (OP 28)

It may not be pure coincidence that rabbit and prunes appear in the same sentence; not only were they both readily available on the pioneer plains but they appear again and again as a traditional combination in general pioneer cookery as well as on Czech menus. The Federal Writers Project files in the Nebraska State Historical Society offer recipes for both Rabbit and Prunes and Rabbit and Sour Cream Gravy:

One rabbit, one half pound of prunes, one-half cup raisins. Boil together until rabbit is tender, season with salt and pepper to taste. Thicken with browned flour.

Wash and salt a jack rabbit. Boil together about 15 minutes a cup of vinegar, a cup of water, one large sliced onion, 2 or 3 bay leaves, a few whole black peppers, a few whole allspice, a piece of ginger, 3 or 4 cloves. Cool and pour over the rabbit. Let it lie thus 3 or 4 days in warm weather or 8 days in cold weather turning it each day. When ready to cook interlard with strips of bacon and place in roaster with piece of butter, two sliced onions, and some of the brine. Turn while roasting and baste with cream. If gravy evaporates, add more liquid or sour cream.

In preparing the manuscript for this book, we had various degrees of difficulty in securing certain recipes. *Wienerschnitzel,* a fairly sophisticated dish, was hard to find in the standard Nebraska pioneer kitchen, for example. We think it is significant that we had no problem at all securing recipes for rabbit with sour cream gravy. Rabbits, prunes, and sour cream were abundant and prunes were cheap and durable. It seems likely therefore that these recipes graced many pioneer tables.

From Jake Hotovy of Lincoln:

Cut up rabbit—season with salt or garlic salt and pepper. Coat with flour or a mixture of flour & some pancake flour. Brown on both sides in skillet. Place in roaster and top with slices of onion. Bake 1½ to 2 hrs depending on size of rabbit at 325° to 350°.

From Adeline Spicka of Clarkson:

When the kids were growing up and both boys went hunting I'd fix the young rabbit this way. Cut up & dredge in flour, salt & pepper to taste. Fry up like spring chicken plus sliced onion added & steamed. Another way just fry pieces without dredging. Salt & pepper & sprinkle with caraway seed & steam.

For large or jack rabbit make a brine of vinegar about 1 part to 3 parts water. Salt about ½ tsp, allspice in small pat (about a teas.) plus 1 large sliced onion. Cook till onion partly done, cool & pour over cut up meat. Cure in cool place about 2 days. Bake an hour or so till tender. Thicken juice to make gravy with flour, add cream if desired. Serve on whole boiled potatoes. Add less vinegar for mild brine.

The hint of cream in that last recipe is a constant theme in rabbit recipes, especially from the Czech kitchens of the Great Plains. From Grandma Anna Horacek of Brainard:

1 cup milk
1 cup water
2 eggs
1 tablespoon vinegar or more

Cook all together. Break or punch a hole in the egg, shake out the contents slowly into boiling liquid mixture. It will look sort of stringy or lumpy, that's what it's supposed to be. Then add about ¼ cup of sour cream

Willa Cather at her rabbit traps during a trip to Virginia

(or a little less). Then mix about 2 level tablespoons flour and enough water to make a thin thickening and stir in the milk & egg mixture. Salt to taste, also add about 2 tablespoons of fresh dill weed, the fine foliage, chopped fine, and cook about 5 min. all together. Best to simmer a bit so gravy does not curdle. Good over fresh fried potatoes.

From Alice Styskal yet another recipe for rabbit (this time, specifically, jackrabbit) with sour-cream gravy and another for fried rabbit:

Wash and salt a cleaned jack rabbit. Make a brine of a cup of vinegar, a cup of water, one large sliced onion, a bit of thyme, two or three bay leaves, a few whole black peppers, a few whole allspice, a piece of ginger and three or four cloves. Boil this brine for at least fifteen minutes. cool and pour over cut up rabbit. Use only an enameled roaster. Keep rabbit in brine for three or four days when weather is warm or at least eight days when weather is cold. Turn meat each day. When ready to cook, take out of brine, and put meat into roaster. Add a little butter, some sliced onion and a little of the brine. Roast, turning frequently. Gravy can be made out of the drippings. Add a little sour cream to the gravy just before serving.

Cut a young rabbit into small pieces. Wash and dry well. Dust with salt, pepper and flour, dip into a beaten egg and then into cracker or bread crumbs. Fry in lard or butter.

Rabbit and squirrel are frequently dismissed as not really being food today. It has always been confusing how we decide what it is we can eat and what it is we cannot. But those determinations are socially and historically deep rooted:

"Ambrosch come along by the cornfield yesterday where I was at work and showed me three prairie dogs he'd shot. He asked me if they was good to eat. I spit and made a face and took on, to scare him, but he just looked like he was smarter'n me and put 'em back in his sack and walked off." . . .

Fuchs put in a cheerful word and said prairie dogs were clean beasts and ought to be good for food, but their family connections were against them. I asked what he meant, and he grinned and said they belonged to the rat family. (MA 71)

Perhaps the most commonly mentioned domesticated meat source in Cather is the chicken. Again, this is scarcely surprising. Chickens are easily raised, they provide eggs as well as meat, and their feathers can be used in comforters. Then, as now, one of the most important parts of a chicken is the wishbone, although in those days there may have been a good many more things to wish for (MA 179). Cather's descriptions of the preparations for a large threshing dinner of chicken is so graphic that it is clear she must have seen many such dinners during her Red Cloud years.

Mahailey wrung the necks of chickens until her wrist swelled up, as she said, "like a puff-adder."

By the end of July the excitement quieted down. The extra leaves were taken out of the dining table, the Wheeler horses had their barn to themselves again, and the reign of terror in the henhouse was over. (OO 138)

In our sermon about hunting we stressed the importance of understanding the sacrifices our fellow creatures make to keep us alive, from beef cattle to barley, but the connection was more immediate on Cather's plains, and that, we feel, was all for the better:

> While I was putting my horse away, I heard a rooster squawking. I looked at my watch and sighed; it was three o'clock, and I knew that I must eat him at six. (MA 307)

Chicken was elegant enough that it could be served to the visiting minister (OO 28), at a wedding supper (OO 159), and yet it was ordinary enough that an old rooster with a frozen comb might be spared for a neighbor who was dangerously low on food (MA 71–72). Chicken was roasted (OO 159) or fried (OP 100). It could be served in the country with hot biscuits and plum preserves (NR 97) or in the city with sweet potatoes (OO 32). Leftovers could be served as chicken salad, although it should be noted that this Cather reference does not involve a farm or pioneer kitchen but a train's dining car (OO 167).

From *The White House Cook Book* (p. 83):

> Pick and draw them, wash out well in two or three waters, adding a little soda to the last but one to sweeten it, if there is doubt as to its being fresh. Dry it well with a clean cloth, and fill the crop and body with a stuffing. . . . Lay it in a dripping pan; put a pint of hot water and a piece of butter in the dripping pan, add to it a small tablespoon of salt, and a small teaspoonful of pepper; baste frequently, and let it roast quickly, without scorching; when nearly done, put a piece of butter the size of a large egg to the water in the pan; when it melts, baste with it, dredge a little flour over, baste again, and let it finish; half an hour will roast a full-grown chicken, if the fire is right. When done, take it up.
>
> Having stewed the necks, gizzards, livers and hearts in a very little water, strain it and mix it hot with the gravy that has dripped from the fowls, and which must be first skimmed. Thicken it with a little browned flour, add to it the livers, hearts and gizzards chopped and small. Or, put the giblets in the pan with the chicken and let them roast. Send the fowls to the table with the gravy in a boat. Cranberry sauce should accompany them, or any tart sauce.

Marked clearly as a favorite recipe in the Cathers' copy of Mrs. Lea's *Domestic Cookery* (p. 23) is this stuffing recipe:

Stuffing for poultry is made of bread and butter, an egg, salt, pepper, chopped parsley or thyme, mixed together; if the bread is dry, it should have a little boiling water poured on it.

Linda has strong memories of farm days in Butler County, Nebraska, when it was time to butcher chickens:

We kids always worked hard those days. There was commotion, blood and squawking, viewed matter of factly and yet with regard for the necessity of eating.

Cleaning day at Aunt Virgie's (Virginia Hoffbauer) farm consisted of tubs of boiling water, cold water, tables and a fire all set up in the barnyard. Enough kids and cousins were rounded up to clean the 30, 60, or 100 chickens we had to clean that day. An aunt with strong hands would cut each chicken's throat with a butcher knife. Even the littlest child would be assigned to watch where the flopping hens came to rest and bring them in. The hens would be scalded in boiling water and laid on the table. The older children would strip off the feathers when cool, saving them for comforters (pesina), feather dusters (perotky) and pillows.

The birds thus unadorned, would be singed (to burn off the pin feathers) with a newspaper rolled into a cone and set afire. Then the poor things would be put into tubs of very cold water to soak and to keep until wrapping time.

Meanwhile in the house an aunt would be organizing dinner, cutting up 3 or 4 of the fresh-killed birds. The chickens were rolled in flour and fried in very hot lard. Gravy was made from the drippings with potato water and milk added. And for some reason, fried chicken, freshly killed, was ever so much better than that from the freezer or store.

Linda's recipe for chicken soup:

Boil cut up chicken until tender enough to debone. Put meat and strained liquid back in pot. Simmer with potatoes, carrots, a whole onion until done. Can add egg noodles toward end.

In addition to turkey and chicken, roast goose is mentioned in Cather's writing. In *My Ántonia,* for example, it is noted that Mrs.

Shimerda used her down comforter to keep coffeecake warm for dinner and had even been known to use it to cover a roast goose (MA 121), and in a later passage Ántonia carves two geese that have been stuffed with apples (MA 360).

From *The White House Cook Book* (pp. 82–83):

> The goose should not be more than eight months old, and the fatter the more tender and juicy the meat. Stuff with the following mixture: Three pints of bread crumbs, six ounces of butter, or part butter and part salt pork, one teaspoonful each of sage, black pepper and salt, one chopped onion. Do not stuff very full, and stitch openings firmly together to keep flavor in and fat out. Place in a baking pan with a little water, and baste frequently with salt and water (some add vinegar); turn often so that the sides and back may be nicely brown. Bake two hours or more; when done take from pan, pour off the fat, and to the brown gravy left add the chopped giblets which have previously been stewed until tender, together with the water they were boiled in; thicken with a little flour and butter rubbed together, bring to a boil and serve. English Style.

The most frequently mentioned pioneer technique for storing meat was "lard packing." Pork, less frequently beef, was fried or boiled in large cauldrons immediately upon butchering (which was usually done shortly after the first of the year). Meat was put in layers in large crocks or barrels, melted fat or tallow being poured over each layer until the container was full. The containers were then put in a cellar or partly buried in the ground, where it would be cool. A crockery, wooden, or cloth cover was set tightly on the meat-filled container; sometimes it was sealed with a thick layer of melted wax.

As the family needed meat it was pried from the lard in the barrel and hot fat was poured over the contents to reseal them. The lard could be used as shortening in the kitchen or used in making soup.

The pioneer family smoked meat, but not to dry it, as was the case with Indian jerky. Inferior cuts of meat were ground up and stuffed into casings (small intestines) to be hung in the smokehouse over a maple, hickory, apple, or (more often on the plains) cob fire. Eight to fifteen parts of pork were mixed with one part beef or venison, with a light addition of salt, pepper, or wild sage. Some ethnic groups had special sausages—Germans had blood sausage, Swedes potato sausage, and so forth.

Hams got much the same treatment. The ham was soaked in a strong brine or was rubbed with salt and saltpeter and was then painted with sorghum molasses, or rolled in sugar, and wrapped in cloth, sewn tightly shut, then painted with molasses. For hams a good fire was built in the smokehouse or the meat was braised over a hot fire to form a glaze and seal in the juices.

I like to cure my own hams and bacon, and for that purpose I mix six to eight pounds of curing salt, one to two pounds of brown sugar, one to two cups of molasses, and two ounces of saltpeter thoroughly per hundred pounds of meat—lighter on the salt for bacon and other thinner or small pieces. I rub the hams, loins, and bacon with this mixture, packing it into the meat's cracks and crevices. I then pack the meat tightly in a crock, which I cover and put in a cool place. After twelve to twenty-four hours I take out the smaller cuts, such as the bacon and loin; the hams remain in the brine syrup for another day. When I take out the smaller cuts, I rerub the hams with the stiff brine syrup from the bottom of the crock.

Pioneers might cure their meats for a month like this, which meant the meat could be stored without refrigeration. It would have to be soaked and rinsed to remove some of the salt from it before it was eaten. I freeze my meats, so the salt is really only for flavor, not preservation.

I smoke my hams one to two days over a cold corncob smoke. There is danger in this business of curing one's own hams, I should warn you. You will never be able to go back to commercially treated ham once you have eaten the real thing.

Meats were also canned and pickled. The following process is from the Nebraska State Historical Society's WPA files:

Cut in two ribs or a round beef, or even a fine thick flank, about twenty pounds weight of either, for example. Finely beat in a mortar for this quantity half a pound of bay salt, a quarter pound each of salt-peter and sal prunella, and two hands of juniper-berries; mix them with three pounds of common salt and one pound of coarse sugar, and thoroughly rub the beef all over for a considerable time. Let it lie in a good salting pan, and rub it well with the pickle once a day for at least a fortnight, carefully turning it every time. Take it out, and after drying it well with a coarse cloth, hang it up to the ceiling of a warm kitchen, or in a chimney corner where only a moderate fire is kept, till it becomes properly dried. It may be either boiled as wanted or cut into rashers and boiled; but in the latter case it will always eat much better if previously dipped into boiling water.

When an animal was butchered, little of it was wasted: a pig's feet were pickled, the hide was tanned, intestines were used for sausage casing, blood was used for sausage, and head parts were used for head cheese, which was made of the snout, brains, cleaned ears, and any other scrap parts of the animal, especially those parts with gristle, which made the gelatin that "set" the sausage. In our home we make Czech *jitrnice* (pronounced *yee'-ther-nit-see*) with dried bread and beef added to the mixture.

The WPA files have several recipes for these dishes that made sure nothing of the precious pork was wasted:

Such parts were mixed with three pounds of pork shank, occasionally a couple of pounds of beef. The mixture was boiled and then cooled, often in pans. When it had "set," it was cut into cubes and seasoned with salt and pepper. Hot juice was poured over it and it was put in a pan with a heavy weight to press it. After it had been pressed it was taken out of the cloth and put in a crock with a strong brine and cured to taste.

The files contain a similar recipe for veal, reproduced here as it appears in the files:

Four pounds of veal shank, two pounds of veal, a little whole allspice, a few bay leaves. Cooked with the meat, salt and pepper to suit taste, cook meat until tender, take up and cool. Then chop. Cook juice down to about one and a half quarts, cool and skim off fat. Then add the chopped meat, salt, pepper to juice and let come to a boil. Pour into granite pan and set in a cool place to harden.

Beef was frequently preserved by corning, which has nothing to do with corn, the word referring instead to salt curing. This also is from the Historical Society's WPA files:

Put beef, when killed and dressed, in a weak brine and let it remain therein a week or ten days, to soak all the blood out of it. Then for every one hundred pounds of meat prepare a brine by using nine parts of salt, two pounds of sugar, two ounces of saltpeter, two ounces black pepper, and six gallons of water. Boil and skim this and pour it hot upon the meat after it has been packed in the barrel.

In the spring draw the brine from the barrel by tapping it at the base, scald and skim again, add a little salt and pour it on the meat again while hot. If at any time the brine should begin to smell bad, it should be drawn off, scalded and skimmed and returned while hot as before. By this means beef can be kept in good condition all summer.

In *One of Ours* there is one of those farm disasters that seem to characterize agriculture on the plains. A roof of a hog shed caved in under a heavy load of snow and twelve precious hogs were suffocated. Claude Wheeler is appalled at the idea of butchering them, especially after having had to work the morning through to dig his way down to them, but Mahailey, ever the reflection of domestic frugality, pleads:

"You ain't a-goin' to let all that good hawg-meat go to wase, air you, Mr. Claude? . . . They didn't have no sickness nor nuthin'. Only you'll have to git right at 'em, or the meat won't be healthy." (oo 87)

When Claude's mother excuses him as being too tired to deal with butchering twelve hogs (doing one is a good job for two men), Mahailey offers:

"I could easy cut up one of them hawgs myself. I butchered my own little pig onct, in Virginia. I could save the hams, anyways, and the spare-ribs. We ain't had not spare-ribs for ever so long." (oo 87)

Ribs were usually eaten immediately after butchering, for they took too much space to be stored. On the plains they were rarely barbecued but more often were placed on a bed of sauerkraut and baked. Hams were prized for their keeping quality because once they had been cured and smoked they could serve a family well into the summer months. The same was true of bacon and side meat (oo 223, op 30).

From *The White House Cook Book* (p. 147):

For each hundred pounds of hams, make a pickle of ten pounds of salt, two pounds of brown sugar, two ounces of saltpetre, one ounce of red pepper, and from four to four and a half gallons of water, or just enough to cover the hams, after being packed in a water-tight vessel, or enough salt to make a brine to float a fresh egg high enough, that is to say, out of the water. First rub the hams with common salt and lay them into a tub. Take the above ingredients, put them into a vessel over the fire, and heat it hot, stirring frequently; remove all the scum, allow it to boil ten minutes, let it cool and pour over the meat. After laying in this brine five or six weeks, take out; drain and wipe, and smoke from two to three weeks. Small pieces of bacon may remain in this pickle two weeks, which would be sufficient.

From Mrs. Lea's *Domestic Cookery* (p. 15):

After washing the pork, cut the skin in squares or stripes; season it with salt and pepper, and baste it with salt and water; thicken, and boil up the gravy.

From *Domestic Cookery* (pp. 14–15):

Have a pig of a suitable size, clean it well, and rub the inside with pepper and salt. Make a stuffing of bread, butter, parsley, sage and thyme; if the bread is stale, pour a little boiling water on it; mix altogether; fill the pig, and sew it up with strong thread, put in the skewers, and spit, and tie the feet with twine; have a pint and a half of water in the bottom of the tin kitchen, with a spoonful of lard and a little salt, with this baste it; and turn it, so as each part will have the benefit of the fire. It should be basted until the skin begins to get stiff with the heat of the fire; then grease it all over with butter or lard, and continue to turn it before the fire, but baste no more, or the skin will blister. A pig will take from two to three hours to roast, according to its size; when it is done, pour the water out in a skillet; season it and thicken it with flour and water. To make a hash gravy, put the liver and heart to boil in three pints of water; after they have boiled an hour, chop them very fine, put them back in the pot, and stir in a thickening of flour and water, with salt, pepper, parsley and thyme. Have the gravies in separate tureens on either side of the pig. Apple sauce and cold slaw are almost indispensable with pig.

Today the word *sausage* is almost synonymous with *pork,* but that was not necessarily the case on the pioneer plains. Sausage was made of all manner of meat (venison, poultry, blood, and rabbit) and from things other than meat (potatoes, bread, sauerkraut). It was a salvage food, a method of rescuing the least of the meat cuts and spoiled or difficult foods like stale bread and blood, just as quilting was a way of salvaging scrap cloth. And like the quilt, sausage could become an independent work of art.

Sausage was thought of as a food form of its own, not just a byproduct of meat. We recently heard a story of an old Catholic recluse who survived on sausage, cheese, and bread which he simply left lying on his farm kitchen table. The village priest once dropped by to pay a visit and found the old hermit eating sausage—on a Friday. The priest scolded the old gent despite his argument that sausage isn't really meat at all and announced that he would have to pay a penance: he would have to deliver a load of wood to the parish hall. The next day the old-timer showed up with a load of sawdust. To the priest's objections, he reasoned, "If sausage is meat, then sawdust is wood!" Sausage is found in Cather's works in association with hot biscuits (NR 76) and with waffles (MA 85), but nearly always for breakfast.

From *The White House Cook Book* (p. 147):

> Boil the forehead, ears and feet, and nice scraps trimmed from the hams of a fresh pig until the meet [*sic*] will almost drop from the bones. Then separate the meat from the bones, put it in a large chopping-bowl, and season with pepper, salt, sage, and summer savory. Chop it rather coarsely; put it back into the same kettle it was boiled in, with just enough of the liquor in which it was boiled to prevent its burning; warm it through thoroughly, mixing it well together. Now pour it into a strong muslin bag, press the bag between two flat surfaces, with a heavy weight on top; when cold and solid it can be cut in slices. Good cold, or warmed up in vinegar.

A scrapple recipe from Ella Cather Lewis with the note "Father used to make this for us every winter":

> Brown and drain 2 lbs pork sausage. Combine 1½ cups light cream and 3 cups water—add to sausage and heat to boiling. Add slowly 1½ cups yellow corn meal with pinch of salt. Cook and stir for 5 minutes. Put

into greased loaf pan. Chill for one day. Slice and fry until brown on both sides. Serve hot with maple syrup and butter. My father used to send my mother off to bridge club and make several batches. We ate it all winter. (Wonderful!)

From the kitchen of Adeline Spicka:

Have been using this recipe for many years. For 1 pound ground pork or beef use seasonings Oregano, marjoram, sage, salt, & pepper, dried crushed parsley (optional). Sprinkle generously over the meat & work in, make into rolls and put in freezer to harden a little & slice. Fry till brown on both sides.

From Alice Styskal:

Take five pounds of pork meat which has been minced fine. Pork from the shoulder is good as it is not lean. To this add half a teaspoon of ground ginger, an even teaspoon of sage, a heaping teaspoon of black pepper and two heaping tablespoons of salt. Mix all this together and put in a cool place where it will keep for several days. This can then be fried as meat cakes or if you want, thin it a little with water and stuff into casings.

Cather's kitchens are frequently Czech kitchens, and for Czech cooks "sausage" meant, more often than not, *jitrnice*.

From Grandma Emily Kresse of Brainard:

Take 1 head of a pig (cleaned, also remove teeth, brains, tongue, eyes). Need some pork hocks or other fatty meat. Boil the head in salty water. Put the heart & hocks in there too. Boil pork & beef tongue separately until the outer cover peels off. Throw away the outer cover & water. Take meat off everything and grind up.

Grind up inner part of tongue too. Grind *raw* liver into it too. Make sure it's raw and not cooked.

Add ½ cup ferina or pearled barley (more or less). Add salt, pepper, ½ cup sausage seasoning, and garlic and onions to taste. Have some loaves of *dry* bread ready. Alternate it with meat when grinding. Soak the bread first and squeeze out water. Strain the water from boiling the head, heart & hocks. Add it slowly to the meat-bread mixture. Make as thin as possible. Put in casings. Boil them just till they rise to the surface.

When ready to eat them, fry until browned.

From Darlene Divis of David City:

The tongue, head, & heart from a pork
1 lb pork liver
Salt to taste
2 tsp pepper
¼ tsp ground cloves
2 tsp marjoram
1 head garlic (mashed to a paste. I put in blender and add hot water & blend till liquid)
Bread
2 tablespoons pork sausage seasoning

Boil the meat until soft. Grind after cooked, adding bread to it when grinding. (Grind liver raw.) Add meat & spices. Add enough of the soup to the meat to make a mixture that will pour. Stuff cleaned casings & tie. Boil in the rest of the soup, can add water if not enough of soup. Boil till they rise to the top, stirring occasionally with ladle. Take out & put into cold water. Then dry. Roast before serving them. May be frozen.

Finally, another application of preservation techniques, pickled pork hocks, from Cheri Underwood of Seward:

Cook 2–3 lbs pork hocks in salted water that just covers hocks. Drain. Boil brine:
1 c. vinegar
2 c. water
1 sliced onion
2 tsp whole allspice
Add salt to taste

Pour over meat and seal. I just mix all brine ingredients cold and pour over meat that is put in clean gallon jar & put in frig. Ready to eat in about a week.

Gravy was a popular dish prepared from meat juice, be it pork, beef, poultry, or game. Gravy was served at the evening meal with its associated entree and could also be put on biscuits or toast for breakfast. Cather mentions chicken gravy in *O Pioneers!* (p. 101) and *My Ántonia* (pp. 77–79), where both chicken and rabbit are spoken of as the basis for mushroom gravy in very positive terms:

"It make very much when you cook, like what my mama say. Cook with rabbit, cook with chicken, in the gravy—oh, so good!" (MA 78)

Linda's recipe for chicken gravy:

Remove chicken from pan after frying. Pour off remaining hot fat in pan, leaving in only one or two tablespoons. To this add flour, a little at a time, stirring constantly. This will become a thick paste as you bring it to a boil. Add milk and potato water to desired consistency. Simmer a few minutes.
Gravy can be made the same way from rabbit pan drippings.

The Shimerdas' mushrooms were gathered in a forest in Bohemia, and the lack of forests on the plains certainly limited the gathering of those delectables there. In my reading or my interviews I have never run across pioneer references to mushrooms other than that single vestige of the Old World mentioned by Cather.

Mutton is not mentioned as a food by Cather, and it was not a common entree on the pioneer table. Cather does however speak of the use of mutton tallow as a lotion for soothing cracked hands (MA 67).

The almost total lack of fish on the plains was especially hard on the Scandinavian settlers, and it is a standard motif of plains pioneer literature that women would travel long distances to fish for catfish or carp—scarcely cod, but better than nothing at all. Cather's Mrs. Bergson was no different:

She missed the fish diet of her own country, and twice every summer she sent the boys to the river, twenty miles to the southward, to fish for channel cat. When the children were little she used to load them all into the wagon, the baby in its crib, and go fishing herself. (OP 29)

For some it was the memory of the fish that became the single remnant of civilization—or sanity—that remained when all else had blown away on the prairie wind:

"My grandmother's getting feeble now, and her mind wanders. She's forgot about this country, and thinks she's at home in Norway. She keeps asking mother to take her down to the waterside and the fish market. She craves fish all the time. Whenever I go home I take her canned salmon and mackerel." (MA 239)

For most of the settlers, fish would have to mean preserved fish: smoked, canned, salted, dried (OO 13). Fish would have to be a snack food rather than a main course, and that is precisely the way it is depicted in Cather's writing:

Before [Mr. Harling] went to bed [Mrs. Harling] always got him a lunch of smoked salmon or anchovies and beer. (MA 157)

Jelinek kept rye bread on hand and smoked fish and strong imported cheeses [in his saloon] to please the foreign palate. (MA 217)

Bread and Cakes

It has always struck me as one of the most remarkable things about tradition that what seems the most permanent is often the most fragile and what seems to be the sort of thing that can last only days is often precisely that part of culture that endures endlessly. It took remarkable skill, for example, to build the fine old barns that dot the eastern American landscape, especially the stone ones that were built to last centuries. The barns last for centuries, it is true. But precisely because the barns are so permanent, the skills that it took to build them have been forgotten. Because a barn was built on a farmstead only every six or ten generations, the techniques have been lost.

Then there is bread. There are of course exceptions like Finnish *Hulbröd,* which is baked only once or twice a year and hung in the kitchen rafters on poles where it can be broken off during the year. It has the capacity to last for some time. But bread is generally a short-lived foodstuff. It is eaten, it molds, it gets weevils, it dries up, it goes stale.

It is precisely these reasons that mean bread had to be made again and again, every week in the pioneer household. As a result the techniques for making it were never forgotten and rarely changed. It wasn't much of a chore for a young girl to learn how her mother made bread because she was involved in the process every Wednesday or Saturday all of her life. I remember my father's mother in only three situations: ironing, making bread, and dying. Domestic work was not something in those days that a woman did; it was what a woman was. Even as Claude Wheeler's mother discussed with him the future of his education, her hands and arms were doing the work of the kitchen:

"Mother," he said one morning when he had an opportunity to speak to her alone, "I wish you would let me quit the Temple, and go to the State University."

She looked up from the mass of dough she was kneading. "But why, Claude?" (OO 22–23)

And sometimes every Saturday. Cather knew the pattern well, as can be seen in small details like that concerning her first encounter with Ántonia Shimerda:

and grandmother packed some loaves of Saturday's bread. . . . (MA 19)

Two contradictory forces were at play in the choice of flours for bread. White wheat flour was considered to be desirable because it was considered rare and a delicacy. This attitude can be seen—or perhaps heard—in an old American folksong cited by Cather in *My Ántonia* (p. 159):

"I won't have none of your weevily wheat, and I won't have none of your
    barley,
But I'll take a measure of fine white flour, to make a cake for Charley."

On the other hand, there was always something to be said for the kind of flour and bread that one had always been used to, and in Scandinavia and central and eastern Europe, especially in peasant households, that was likely to be rye flour and rye bread:

"My old folks . . . have put in twenty acres of rye. They get it ground at the mill, and it makes nice bread. It seems like my mother ain't been so homesick, ever since father's raised rye flour for her." (MA 239)

In the pioneer household, Monday was washday, Tuesday for ironing and mending. Wednesday was set aside for baking. Thursday and Friday were for house cleaning and other domestic chores, Saturday was bath day and possibly the rare trip into town. Sunday was for worship, or at any rate, rest.

The flour barrel occupied a central location in the kitchen, cupboard, or cellar (if it was dry enough to store flour in; see OO 19, 217) and the preparation of bread was a part of any meal. A passage in *One of Ours* about the baking for a threshers' dinner is particularly colorful:

Mrs. Wheeler baked pies and cakes and bread loaves as fast as the oven would hold them, and from morning till night the range was stoked like the fire-box of a locomotive. (OO 138)

Baking was not a simple, one time operation. My own grandmother made her dough in a washtub for her family of ten; making a week's supply for such a family was a heroic job, and the stove steamed and breathed its warm, brown aroma hour after hour:

There was baking going on in the Rosicky kitchen all day, and Rosicky sat inside. . . . (NR 94)

Jim Burden and Alexandra speak of women working their bread (MA 68, OP 46), in Burden's case on a board. As was the case with meats, bread could be purchased at a bakery or grocery store (MA 146, 216) and there are passages in Cather's work where one cannot determine for certain whether the bread was "boughten" or homemade (OO 85), but there are others where it is clear though tacit that bread is first of all and best of all homemade (NR 99).

In one passage of *My Ántonia* slovenly bread making is used to delineate more clearly the character of Mrs. Shimerda (at least in this country), but her technique for saving her sour-dough culture is no more primitive than the best cooks' might be:

I remember how horrified we were at the sour, ashy-grey bread she gave her family to eat. She mixed her dough, we discovered, in an old tin peck-measure that Krajiek had used about the barn. When she took the paste out to bake it, she left smears of dough sticking to the sides of the measure, put the measure on the shelf behind the stove and let this residue ferment. The next time she made bread, she scraped this sour stuff down into the fresh dough to serve as yeast. (MA 31)

Circled in the Cather family copy of *The White House Cook Book* (p. 231):

One teacupful of wheat flour, one-half teacupful of salt, one pint of warm water; add sufficient Graham flour to make the dough as stiff as can be stirred with a strong spoon; this is to be mixed at night; in the morning, add one teaspoonful of soda, dissolved in a little water; mix well, and pour into two medium-sized pans; they will be about half full; let it stand in a warm place until it rises to the top of the pans, then bake one hour in a pretty hot oven.

This should be covered about twenty minutes when first put into the oven with a thick brown paper, or an old tin cover; it prevents the upper crust from hardening before the loaf is well risen. If these directions are correctly followed the bread will not be heavy or sodden, as it has been tried for years and never failed.

A recipe for Boston Brown Bread circled and underlined in the same book (p. 232):

One pint of rye flour, one quart of corn meal, one teacupful of Graham flour, all fresh; half a teacupful of molasses or brown sugar, a teaspoonful of salt, and two-thirds of a teacupful of home-made yeast. Mix into as stiff a dough as can be stirred with a spoon, using warm water for wetting. Let it rise several hours, or over night; in the morning, or when light, add a teaspoonful of soda dissolved in a spoonful of warm water [the last phrase is underlined in pencil in the Cather copy]; beat it well, and turn it into well-greased, deep bread-pans, and let it rise again. Bake in a MODERATE oven from three to four hours.

The following recipe for bran bread is handwritten on an Aetna Insurance Company note paper in the pages of the Cather copy of *The White House Cook Book*:

2 cups of bran
2 cups of flour
½ cup of sugar
1 c of raisins

2 t of baking p.

1 t of soda

Salt

One egg

2 T of molasses

2 c of sweet milk

Mix dry ingredients [*sic*] first. Add milk & molasses last. Bake in greased pans ¾ hour in slow oven. Two loves [*sic*].

From a handwritten three-by-five card in the Cathers' *White House Cook Book* comes this recipe for Cinnamon Bread:

1 cup flour

½ " sugar

1 teaspoon cinnamon

½ teaspoonfull bakin [*sic*] powder

1 egg well beaten

2 tablespoon melted butter

½ cup milk

Bake 20 min.

Journey Cake, from Mrs. Lea's *Domestic Cookery* (p. 79):

Pour boiling water on a quart of meal, put in a little lard and salt, and mix it well; have an oak board with a rim of iron at the bottom, and an iron handle fastened to it that will prop it up to the fire; put some of the dough on it, dip your hand in cold water and smooth it over; score it with a knife, and set it before coals to bake.

Virginia Pone, from *Domestic Cookery* (p. 80):

Beat three eggs, and stir them in a quart of milk, with a little salt, a spoonful of melted butter, and as much sifted corn meal as will make it as thick as corn batter cakes; grease the pan and bake quick.

Indian Bread, from the same source (p. 80):

To one quart of butter-milk, slightly warmed, put a tea-spoonful of salaeratus [*sic*], dissolved in water, two eggs, well beaten, a table-spoonful of melted butter or lard, a little salt; stir in with a spoon as much Indian meal as will take a thick batter; beat it for a few minutes, grease your pans, and bake quickly. If you bake this quantity in two pans, a half hour will be sufficient, or if in one, it will take an hour. Look at it often while baking, as it is liable to burn. An excellent recipe.

A handwritten recipe for cornbread found in the Cather's *White House Cook Book*:

1 cup of corn meal
½ cup of flour
1 heaping teaspoon baking powder
1 egg (beaten)
1 cup of sweet milk
1 tablespoon of sugar
1 teaspoon of salt
1 tablespoon of corn oil or melted butter
Directions: Beat the egg, add the milk. Sift in the meal, flour etc. Add butter last.

Two yeast recipes are circled in the Cather copies of *The Home Queen Cook Book*; the first has no pagination, the second is on page 258:

Pare and grate 12 large potatoes, add 1 tea-cup sugar and ½ cup salt. Boil 2 handfuls of hops in 1 gallon of water five minutes, and strain onto the other ingredients. Put the mixture into a tin pail and set in kettle of boiling water and stir till it thickens. When cooked add 1 pt. of good sweet yeast, or 4 fresh yeast cakes. Stir well, cover up tight, and set in a warm place to rise. When light, put into stone or glass jar and set in a cool place in the cellar. Use ½ cup of this yeast for two loaves of bread.

Boil a handful of hops in 2 qts. of water and strain. Grate 6 large potatoes, add 1 large spoon salt, 1 large spoon flour, 2 large spoons sugar; put all together and let come to boil; when about cool stir in 1 tea-cup yeast and keep in a warm place to raise well, after which it may be bottled and kept 6 weeks more. One cup should be kept each time to start fresh. Always reliable.

Bread was eaten with molasses (MA 124) and meat drippings (NR 99, but in reference to England). And we have a subtle reference to ingredients of Czech-style breads in a passage dealing with Mrs. Shimerda's bread:

I . . . went into the kitchen where Mrs. Shimerda was baking bread, chewing poppy seeds as she worked. (MA 121)

As I read this passage I cannot help but recall a comment by a friend who defined Czech cooking as "regular food, but with poppy seeds."

Even more common than passages about bread in Cather's prairie pioneer works are those about biscuits. Combinations of biscuits and sausages at breakfast predominate (for example, NR 75). Boughten bread and white bread came to be recognized as the elegant thing to eat at supper—in contrast to those rich, dark, heavy peasant breads I love so much. In *My Ántonia* the Widow Steavens even makes the attitude explicit:

"You've no prejudice against hot biscuit for supper? Some have, these days." (MA 307)

But when they sit down to less-fancy suppers, Cather's characters still reach for the biscuits (OO 139).

A biscuit recipe taken from a side panel of a Dwight's Cow Brand Soda box is found in the pages of the Cather family copy of *The Home Queen Cook Book*:

Take one quart of flour, one tablespoonful of salt and a small teaspoonful of Dwight's Cow Brand Soda, sift thoroughly together, then rub in a heaping teaspoonful of lard or butter and add sufficient sour milk or buttermilk to make a soft dough—just stiff enough to handle with the floured hand. Roll out the dough and cut out the biscuits. Have the oven and pans hot and bake immediately.

A marked recipe for Breakfast Muffins is on page 286 of *The Home Queen Cook Book*:

One pt. flour, 1 cup sweet milk, 2 eggs beaten light, scant ½ cup butter, scant ½ cup sugar, 2 tea-spoons baking powder. Bake in patty, or gem tins.

From the same source, page 286:

One pt. sweet milk, 3 eggs well beaten, 1 cup flour, a little salt. Bake in a quick oven.

From a handwritten note found between the pages of *The Home Queen Cook Book*:

¼ cup butter
⅓ cup sugar
1 egg
2⅔ cups flour
4 teaspoons b. f. [bran flour?]
½ teaspoon salt
1 cup milk
1 cup berries

Cream the butter, add sugar & egg well beaten, mix & sift flour, baking powder & salt, reserving one fourth cup flour to be mixed with berries & added last.

Handwritten Bran Jem (gem) recipe found in pages of *The Home Queen Cook Book*:

1½ cup bran
½ ″ white flour [*sic*] (2 cups graham)
¼ c molasses
¼ c chopped nuts & raisins
¼ c butter (melted)
1 egg
1½ cup sour milk
1 larg [*sic*] teaspoon soda

Put in hot pans & bake fast 20 min to ½ hr.

The lines below immediately follow the recipe above but appear to be a different recipe:

1 egg
4 tablespoon butter
1 cup sugar
1½ cup flour
2½ T b.f. [bran flour?]
½ cup milk
½ T of cinnamon
1½ T of sugar on top
Bits of butter on top
Shallow pan

Dark breads and other strong-tasting European delicacies were reserved for the peasant table and for the tavern, "where the Bohemian and German farmers could eat the lunches they brought from home while they drank their beer" (MA 217).

Rye bread from the kitchen of Virginia Hoffbauer of rural Butler County:

Mix in large bowl:

6 cups lukewarm water

¾ cup sugar

3 tbsp salt

Crumble in 2 cakes yeast or fresh yeast. Stir until yeast is well dissolved. Add:

6 tbsp soft shortening

2 tbsp caraway (optional)

Mix in 7 to 8 cups flour and stir very well. Add 4 cups pure rye flour and enough white flour to make easy to handle. Turn out on slightly floured board and knead until smooth. Place in greased bowl, turning once. Bring greased side up. Cover with waxed paper and then tea towel. Let rise until doubled.

Turn out on greased board. Cut and shape. Let rise till light. Bake at 350° about 40 minutes. Makes 6 loaves.

Cather rephrases the familiar adage "The grass is always greener on the other side of the fence" in terms of bread:

Swedes [like] to buy Danish bread and the Danes [like] to buy Swedish bread, because people always think the bread of another country is better than their own. (OP 62–63)

A Danish rye bread from the very Scandinavian kitchen of Harriett Nielsen of Dannebrog:

Dissolve 1 pkg yeast in ½ cup lukewarm water & add 1 tsp sugar. In a saucepan, scald 1½ c buttermilk, 1½ c water. Take off stove and add ½ cup (scant) shortening. Crisco or bacon grease is fine. ½ c molasses, scant tablespoon salt, 3 cups rye graham flour. This should be lukewarm now, so add yeast mixture and beat well. Let rise about 1 hr. Then add 4 or more cups white flour, enough so it doesn't stick to hands. Grease bowl, turn to grease top and let rise about double. Make into four loaves. Poke the top about 14 times each loaf with a knife or fork. Cover and let rise (not double or it will be crumbly). Bake 375° about 45 min. When you take it out, grease the top with butter.

A Swedish rye from the same source:

> 5 cups lukewarm water
> 4 teaspoons salt
> ½ cup brown sugar
> 4 cups rye flour
> 10–12 cups white flour (sifted)
> 2 pkgs cake yeast or 2 tablespoons active dry yeast
> 1 cup molasses
> 1 cup vegetable oil

Combine rye flour, sugar, salt and water. Beat well. Add yeast which has been dissolved in ½ cup of lukewarm water. Stir into mixture well. Let stand in warm place until it rises double in bulk; then add molasses and vegetable oil and white flour. Knead well. Cover and let rise double in bulk. Work down lightly and let rise again. Make into 8 loaves and let rise double in bulk. Bake in pre-heated oven 350° for 40–45 minutes. Freezes well.

And there are nut breads (NR 78). This one is from a handwritten note found in the pages of the Cathers' *White House Cook Book*:

> 2 cups graham flour
> 2 cups white flour
> 2 cups milk
> 1 cup sugar
> As many nuts as you like
> Teaspoon salt
> Three teaspoons baking powder
> Mix and put in pan. Let rise for twenty minutes. Bake.

I think it is wonderful that, with all the speculators' dreams and schemes for wealth, it is Tiny Soderball of *My Ántonia* who hits it rich, and her secret is bread:

Two days later Tiny and her friends, and nearly everyone else in Circle City, started for the Klondike fields on the last steamer that went up the Yukon before it froze for the winter. That boatload of people founded Dawson City. Within a few weeks there were fifteen hundred homeless men in camp. Tiny and the carpenter's wife began to cook for them, in a tent. The miners gave her a building lot, and the carpenter put up a log hotel for her. There she sometimes fed a hundred and fifty men a day. Miners came in on snowshoes from their placer claims twenty miles away to buy fresh bread from her, and paid for it in gold. (MA 300)

Today's plainsmen may think of doughnuts as being a modern and very American food, but among my German-Russian people a fried dough coated with sugar and called *Grebel* is a traditional food, especially for Good Friday. As a child I was in charge of taking the hot *Grebel* and dropping them into a brown paper sack containing a couple of cups of sugar. I would vigorously shake two or three *Grebel* in the sack, coating them with the confection, and then I would put them on a plate. Most of them. About one of every three, as I recall, I ate.

Later when I worked among the Omaha Indians in Lincoln, I saw that familiar, irregular shape of quickly cut dough and the color of lard-fried bread make its appearance at Omaha hand games, pow-wows, and prayer meetings. Fried bread is a popular old-time dish because it makes possible the preparation of bread in a simple frying pan rather than a complicated oven; although its introduction to Plains Indian cuisine is quite recent, it is thought of as a thoroughly Indian foodstuff.

For Cather, sandwiches and doughnuts were a quick meal for winter travelers (MA 51–52) and the foundation for a leisurely, opulent meal on Sunday, when even the hired help lounged around in bed until 7 A.M. (OO 17).

Elsie Cather's doughnuts, from a handwritten note in *The White House Cook Book*:

1 big cup of sugar
1 scant cup of sweet milk
2 eggs
2 heaping tablespoons of melted butter
2 heaping teaspoons of baking powder
Flour enough to mix
beat sugar & eggs to cream   add milk gradually   add butter gradu-

ally   sift about ½ flour   then add the rest   beat well   work dough so as
to handle nicely   big   ½ thick   turn when first they come to the top &
then turn a second time

    3 lbs hot lard

    Grate nutmeg into powed [*sic*] sugar & then power [*sic*]

A recipe for doughnuts from a handwritten note found in Mrs.
Lea's *Domestic Cookery*:

    3 tablespoonsful of lard
    1 cup sour milk
    2 eggs
    ½ cup sugar
    Cinamon [*sic*] & alspice [*sic*]
    A little soda & salt
    Mrs. Perkins

I feel warmest toward Cather when she uses clear and un-
mistakable references to ethnic foods—ethnic *peasant* foods. The
theme of *My Ántonia* is the triumph of honest peasantry, its nobility.
One of the most important things about the book is that it lauds the
noble savage without falling into the maudlin and melodramatic
failings of most Romantics. As a Romantic myself, I find Cather
most appealing when she is herself a Romantic. Few literary scholars and historians today like to grant that Cather was ever a Romantic, but she was at her best, and only at her best, when she indulged
herself in honest, homely passions and pursued her writing with
emotion as well as skill. The sadness in those works however is
obvious evidence of Cather's regret for having tasted the apple of
rural peasant life and having eventually lost the fulfillment of that
honesty herself. In my opinion, she crowned her literary achieve-
ment when she perceived, appreciated, and shared the power of
Ántonia's simple fulfillment in motherhood, domesticity, farming,
and union with a loved mate with an audience: us.

    All of which is to introduce coffeecake and *kolaches*. I will not
apologize that I am attracted to those passages because of resonances
from my own childhood, where *Dienekuche* and *Riegelkuche* were so

special a treat that I can still taste them at this very moment. (Have you ever noticed how difficult it is to recall a taste memory? Imagine, then, what an impression those things have made on me in this life.) I wonder how my mother made those little crumbly nuggets on the top of the coffeecake. I suppose I could ask her, but I prefer to believe it was magic.

Now my life is filled with *kolaches,* for I have married a Czech peasant woman, another Ántonia, who is never satisfied to make a dozen or two but always makes several hundred so she can strew the neighborhood and family across the city, if not eastern Nebraska, with bundles of six or ten. At the moment she has out IOUs for *kolaches* to Buzz at the service station for dropping everything to fix something or another that went wrong with her car one day, and to my father for painting a chair, and to her brother Mike for some family photographs he took. It always amazes me that one day our kitchen can be filled at every corner with *kolaches* and the next day there isn't one left for my lunch.

While others have attributed America's power and wealth to natural resources, God's will, singleness of purpose, or superior economic system, I have always thought that it is the inevitable American mixing of gene pools and recipe files. Such beautiful children come from unions between Omahas and Swedes, Greeks and Mexicans, Germans and Czechs. Such beautiful tables of food come from families where there is no embarrassment about fundamental origins and where cultures have come together to offer up the best of children and food.

For me, coffeecake was always just that: cake for coffee, for breakfast or afternoon coffee. I was therefore surprised to find Mrs. Shimerda cooking a coffeecake in the afternoon, to be served at supper (MA 121). It was seen, perhaps, as an elegant finish to what is a decidedly humble meal, perhaps even a famine meal:

we sat down at the oilcloth-covered table. Mrs. Shimerda ladled meal mush out of an iron pot and poured milk on it. After the mush we had fresh bread and sorghum molasses, and coffee with the cake that had been kept warm in the feathers [that is, the feather comforter]. (MA 124)

Marie, who is reputed to be able to make a dozen kinds of bread (OP 194), offers her company coffeecake with nuts and poppy seeds, with a topping of rich farm cream. There also is mention of a nut cake in *My Ántonia* on page 155.

The following coffeecake recipe is from a handwritten note found in the pages of *The White House Cook Book*:

> 1 cup powdered sugar
> 5 egg yolks beat together 15 minutes
> 1½ tablespoon coffee ext.
> 1 cup flour
> 1 teaspoon baking powder
> Whites of 5 eggs

[An unidentifiable word follows *eggs* above. It looks like *loset, losel,* or *loseby.* Perhaps *loosely,* as "beaten loosely."]

> FROSTING
> ½ pint cream whip
> ½ tablespoon coffee ext
> 1 tablespoon sugar [three totally unidentifiable words follow the word *sugar*]
> 1 cup powdered sugar
> 1½ tablespoon coffee extract if stiff add little water

From a handwritten note found between the pages of the Cathers' *Domestic Cookery*:

> 1 cup powdered suger [*sic*]
> Yolks 5 egg—beat 15 mi.
> 2 tablespoons coffee extract
> 1 cup flour
> 1 teaspoon baking powder
> Whites of [number totally and unfortunately obliterated] eggs

> [word blurred, but probably *filling*]
> ½ pt cream whipped stiff
> 2 tablespoon coffee [probably *extract*]
> 2 tablespoon sugar

TOP
1 cup powdered sugar
2 tablespoon coffee E.

Two coffeecake recipes marked in *The Home Queen Cook Book* (p. 332):

One cup sugar, 1 cup butter, 1 cup molasses, 1 cup chopped raisins, 4 cups flour, 1 cup strong coffee, 1 tea-spoon cinnamon, ½ nutmeg. Bake slowly.

One cup sugar, 2 cups molasses, 1 cup butter, ½ cup strong coffee, 1 lb. Raisins, 1 lb. citron, 1 egg, 1 tea-spoon soda, spice to taste.

From a clipping cut from *Demorest's Monthly Magazine* and placed between the pages of *The Home Queen Cook Book*:

Eggs . . . two
Sugar . . . " cups
Flour . . . four   "
Raisins . . . one-half pound
Currants . . .   "   "
Cinnamon . . . two teaspoonfuls
Mace . . .   "   "
Allspice . . .   "   "
Strong cold coffee . . . one cup
Saleratus . . . one teaspoonful
Dissolve the saleratus in the coffee; mix the ingredients, and bake slowly.

In this same passage (OP 194) and two others coffeecake is part of a commonplace phrase: "coffeecake and *kolaches*" (NR 82, 99, OP 193–95). Marie offers the combination to her guests with an explanation:

"The Bohemians always like them with their coffee. But if you don't, I have a coffee-cake with nuts and poppy seeds." (OP 194)

It is Mrs. Lee's aesthetic judgments of the *kolaches* in this passage that charms me most:

Mrs. Lee held up one of the apricot rolls between her brown thumb and forefinger and weighed it critically. "Yust like-a fedders," she pronounced with satisfaction. "My, a-an't dis nice!" (OP 195)

Marie's *kolaches* were stuffed with stewed apricots and Ántonia's with spiced plums (MA 338), but my favorite have always been those with poppy seeds. While Cather has her Czech cooks making bread with poppy seeds, they are unfortunately not mentioned specifically in connection with *kolaches*. I'll just assume that Ántonia's *kolaches* in the supper passage late in *My Ántonia* (MA 346–47) were filled with poppy seeds.

Although *kolaches* were not a part of Cather's home kitchen, she certainly understood their central position in the Czech kitchens she visited and wrote about. If not, would she have written elsewhere: "If security could ever have a smell, it would be the fragrance of a warm *kolache*" or "I could name a dozen Bohemian towns in Nebraska where one used to be able to go into a bakery and buy better pastry than is to be had anywhere except in the best pastry shops of Prague or Vienna"?

We found no recipes for *kolaches* in the Cather files, but that isn't surprising: they were a part of the Czech kitchens she visited and described rather than those in which she grew up. We have therefore turned to the Bohemian cooks of our own experience for the recipes that follow.

From Virginia Hoffbauer:

2 c warm milk, let cool before adding yeast
½ cup sugar generous
2 tsp salt
½ cup oleo or lard
2 eggs beaten
Mix well in bowl, add flour, 2 cups
Add to bowl 2 pkgs dry yeast soaked in ½ c warm water and some sugar and flour. Mix another 2 cups till smooth and soft. Add another cup of flour until sticky. Flour table to make rolls on. Dust top with flour. Then grease sides of bowl with your hand. Dip into bowl of grease & whip

outside in. Set in sink of warm water, cover. Let rise half then punch. Oil on hands, turn dough, then work making buns & let rise again. Push out center & fill with filling. Let rise a little again. Grease pans. Bake at 350°.

From our own kitchen:

3 pkg. dry yeast
¾ cup lukewarm water
¾ cup shortening
1 cup sugar
3 tsp salt
2¼ cups milk (heated)
3 beaten eggs
Lots of flour
Bowl of grease (½ cup)
(must use wooden spoon to mix)

Dissolve yeast in water & a little sugar. Combine shortening, sugar, salt, and the hot milk. Let cool. Mix in 3 beaten eggs and yeast (make sure it's good). Add two cups flour and mix until smooth. Keep adding flour until smooth and soft. Keep adding until dough is sticky. Dip hands in bowl of grease and grease sides of bowl (with dough) with your hands. Whip outside in and grease bottom of bowl too. Dust top of dough with flour. Cover and let rise half again or more. Grease hands and punch dough down. Let rise again. Then make pingpong ball size dough on greased pans. Let rise. Push out center and fill with filling. Let rise. Bake at 350° until browned. Brush dough with butter after they come out of the oven.

Prune Filling: Cook 2 pounds of dry fruit (add some raisins too if you have them) in enough water to cover until tender. Drain & pit (if cooking prunes). Mash well. Add 1 cup sugar, 1 tsp. vanilla and ¼ tsp cinnamon. I like to make this the night before and reheat it when I bake.

Kolache dough is remarkably versatile and is used for several other traditional Czech breads. From Grandma Emily Kresse of Butler County:

(Doughnuts) Start with ping-pong ball size pieces of dough. Pinch big hole in center, drop into hot grease. Turn when brown. Drain on paper toweling. Coat anytime with sugar.

(Horns) Make hand balls, same as doughnuts. Roll out one side, turn, do the other. Roll, pinch ends and put on greased pan. Brush with butter before baking.

(Cinnamon rolls) Flour table. Roll out dough thin. Put goodly amount of sugar/cinnamon on and big clumps of brown sugar. Roll into tight roll. Cut off pieces. Set side up. Brush with oil in between rolls so they don't stick together while baking.

My Ántonia has three passages that mention gingerbread. They are all early in the book and associated with Christmas. One (MA 9) is simply a mention of the smell of the bread baking, but the others (MA 81, 82) offer more of an understanding of the form the gingerbread was to take for the festivities. One (MA 82) describes the bread's being cut into animal forms, and in the other:

Grandmother hunted up her fancy cake-cutters and baked gingerbread men and roosters, which we decorated with burnt sugar and red cinnamon drops. (MA 81)

Cakes appear frequently in Cather as a dessert. Cake occurs occasionally simply as a category of confection, often as a complement for pies (MA 39, 66; OP 133), but other passages are quite explicit and varied in the types of cake at hand. There is apple cake (NR 90), sugar cake (MA 110), chocolate cake (MA 113), chocolate cake with icing (MA 111), and angel food cake (OO 107).

This recipe for Marble Cake is from an undated, unidentified printed-item note pasted to the endboards of the Cathers' copy of Mrs. Lea's *Domestic Cookery*:

Half a cupful of molasses; ½ cupful of sugar; ½ cupful of butter; ½ cupful of buttermilk; 3 cupfuls of flour; 2 eggs; ½ pound of raisins (cut lengthwise with the shears); One teaspoonful each of cinnamon, allspice and cloves; ½ teaspoonful of soda; ½ of a nutmeg. For the light, take 1½ cupfuls of white sugar, ¾ cupful of butter; ¾ cupful of sweet milk; 3 cupfuls of flour; whites of 3 eggs; 1 teaspoonful of lemon extract; 1½ teaspoonfuls of cream of tartar, and ⅔ teaspoonful of soda.

Gussie Thomas

Spice Cake, also from a handwritten note in *Domestic Cookery*:

1 cup brown sugar
½ cup of butter
2 eggs
1 cup molasses
1 cup sour milk & a little soda
Heaping teaspoonfull of cloves, Cinnamon, a little nutmeg, 2 or 3 teaspoonful [*sic*] of grated chocalate [*sic*], 3 cups of flour, a few raisins.

Apple Jelly Cake, from yet another handwritten note in *Domestic Cookery*:

FILLING
Pare and grate three apples
⅔ cup of sugar
1 beaten egg
Mix all and cook, stirring constantly. When done and cooled flavor with lemon or vanilla

CAKE
3 eggs beaten whites and yolks
½ cup sugar
½ cup butter
2 cup milk
Sift three cups of flour with two teaspoonfuls of baking powder. Mix and divide baking in sheets. Use jelly while hot.

Another cake—Honey Cake—from a handwritten note in *The White House Cook Book*:

1½ cups honey
1¾ cups sour milk
½ cup butter or catosuet [or perhaps *cotosuet* or *catasuet*]
3 eggs
1 cup rice flour
1½ wheat flour
1 teaspoon baking powder
1 teaspoon soda

Flavor with mapleine [*sic*]
2 ciny. [*sic*]
1 large cup Karo
Whites of 1 eggs
Cook Karo until hairs well [strings fine]

Mahogany Cake, from a handwritten note in *The White House Cook Book*:

1½ c sugar
½ c butter
½ c sweet milk
2 c flour
3 eggs
1 tea-spoon of soda dissolved in a little milk
Vanilla
½ c chocolate cooked in ½ c. milk. Cool & stir in before the flour

FILLING
1½ c sugar cooken /?/ in
½ c milk. Beat until cool.

Hickory Nut Cake, from the recipe file of Mrs. Jennie Miner Reiher. This was a Cather family favorite that Annie Pavelka (Ántonia) made for them when she worked there:

1½ cups powdered sugar
½ cup butter
2 cups flour
2 tsp baking powder
⅔ cup water
1 tsp vanilla
4 egg whites
⅔ cup nuts, chopped

Cream sugar and butter together until fluffy. Sift together flour and baking powder. Add alternating to creamed mixture with water. Add vanilla and fold in stiffly beaten egg whites. Add nut meats and bake in greased loaf pan or 2 layer pans. Bake at 350 degrees, 50–55 minutes for the loaf, 25–30 minutes for layers. Frost with boiled icing or use whipped cream.

Aunt Jennie's Almond Squares: Cut hickory cake into squares. Roll in almonds that are shelled, blanched, toasted, and crushed. Powder and roll in one cupful of nut meats. Bake in steady oven.

Walnut Cake, from the same source:

One cupful sugar, one-half cupful each butter and milk, two eggs, one teaspoonful cream tartar, one-half teaspoonful soda, one cupful walnuts, chopped fine; one-half cupful each raisins and currants, two cupfuls flour.

The following Nut Cake recipe is from an undated and untitled newspaper clipping found in the pages of *The Home Queen Cook Book*:

Cream one cup of butter with two cups of sugar, add four beaten eggs, one cup of cold water and three cups of flour that has been sifted with three teaspoonfuls of baking powder. Last of all, stir in two cups of nut meats, well dredged with flour.

This recipe for Gold Cake is from a printed but unidentified sheet folded within the pages of *The Home Queen Cook Book*:

Yolks of 8 eggs, 1 cup granulated sugar, ¼ cup butter, ½ cup sweet milk, 1½ cups flour, 2 teaspoonsful of baking powder. Cream butter and sugar together. Beat the yolks thoroughly, and stir in butter and sugar, put in milk, then flour and stir hard. Bake in tube loaf about forty minutes.

Solid Chocolate Cake, from the same sheet as the recipe above:

1¾ cups sugar, 2 eggs, ¼ cup butter, ½ cup sweet milk, 2 cups flour, 3 teaspoonsful baking powder, ½ cake of chocolate dissolved in ½ cup boiling water. Put in chocolate the last thing; flavor to suit.

Banana Spice Cupcakes from Emily Kresse, a favorite in her family:

Combine 1–3 cups well mashed ripe bananas, teaspoon lemon juice
Sift together 1–3 times:
2¼ cups sifted flour
2 tsp double acting baking powder
½ tsp soda

1 tsp salt
1½ cups sugar
1 tsp nutmeg
Add ½ cup shortening
⅔ cup evaporated milk (soured with 2 tbs vinegar)
add the mashed bananas
Beat 2 minutes at medium or 300 strokes
Add 2 eggs, unbeaten, 1 tsp vanilla
Beat 1 minute
Fill cupcake papers and bake at 350° or 375° 25–30 minutes
Chocolate frosting:
1 cup sugar
Moisten with canned milk. Heat to boil and stir. Add cocoa. Can add butter so it won't crack.

If numbers are an indication, cakes were a very important part of the Cather diet. Marked recipes in the cookbooks, printed recipes from magazines, and handwritten recipes for cakes constitute a remarkably large proportion of the family's files. This recipe for Fudge Cake was handwritten on a school spelling form and was found in *The White House Cook Book*:

1 c sugar
1 c sour cream
1½ c flour
½ teaspoon of soda in cream
½ teaspoon b. powder in flour
2 eggs
1 square chocolate
Salt & spice to taste

FILLING
Boil for six minutes
2 sq chocolate
1 c sugar
⅓ c milk
Add two tbs. butter
Boil another six min.

Flavor & beat.
Add nuts if desired.

The following handwritten recipe, found in *The Home Queen Cook Book,* was labeled "Mrs. Spoke Fields Sponge Cake":

5 eggs beaten seperately [*sic*]
1½ cup of sugar
1½ cup of flour
1 tablespoon of baking powder
Half cup of boiling water

A Sponge Cake, from page 326 of *The Home Queen Cook Book,* where it is circled in pencil:

Four eggs, 2 cups sifted flour, 2 cups granulated sugar, 2 level teaspoons baking powder, 1 cup hot water almost boiling. Beat yolks and whites of eggs together very lightly, add the sugar, then 1 cup of flour a little at a time, put the baking powder in the other cup, lastly the hot water little by little—the batter is very thin—bake in dripping pan about 25 minutes.

And a Warm Sponge Cake from page 327 of *The Home Queen Cook Book,* where it is bracketed, x-ed, and underlined!

Four eggs, 1 cup sugar, 1 cup flour, 1 tea-spoon baking powder, salt, lemon flavor.

All three of the following nut cake recipes are from the Cathers' *Home Queen Cook Book* (p. 340):

Whites of 4 eggs, 1½ cups sugar, ½ cups butter, ¾ cup sweet milk, 1½ cup chopped nut, not too fine (walnuts or almonds), 2 tea-spoons baking powder, 1½ cups sifted flour. Frost and put whole nuts on top.

Two cups sugar, 1 cup butter, 3 cups flour, 1 cup milk, 4 eggs, 2 teaspoons baking powder, 1 cup nut meats cut fine (hickory nuts are very nice), ½ tea-spoon extract almond.

Take ½ cup butter, 1 cup milk, 4 eggs, 2 tea-spoons baking powder, 2 cups sugar, 3 cups flour, 1 pt. nut meats. Cream butter and sugar, add eggs well whipped, milk, flour, with baking powder, and nut meats chopped fine. Bake in loaf. English walnuts are best.

This handwritten recipe for Nut Cake was found between the pages of *The White House Cook Book*:

1 cup sugar
½ cup butter
whites of 3 eggs
½ cup sweet milk
1 large cup Eng. walnuts
BLOW OFF SKINS
6 teaspoons B.P. [probably baking powder]

The next three recipes are from a long article in the January, 1910, issue of *The People's Home Journal,* titled "Cake Making and Baking," by Beatrice D'Emo, and were found in the pages of the Cathers' *White House Cook Book*:

HICKORY NUT LAYER CAKE WITH CHOCOLATE ICING

Half a cupful of butter, one and one-half cupfuls of granulated sugar, three-quarters of a cupful of water, two and one-quarter cupfuls of flour, a pinch of salt, two level teaspoonfuls of baking powder, the whites of four eggs, one cupful of chopped hickory-nut meats. Bake in rather thick layers, using only two to a cake, and frost with the glossy chocolate icing, decorating with the halves of hickory nut meats placed in fancy pattern before the icing hardens. English walnuts may be used instead of the hickory nuts.

GLOSSY CHOCOLATE FROSTING

Cook one and one-half cupfuls of granulated sugar with five table-spoonfuls of milk until it forms a syrup, being careful that it does not scorch; then add two ounces of chocolate which has been melted with a tablespoonful of milk and pour over the whites of two eggs (beating hard all the time). Flavor when cool, and do not touch after pouring over the cake until it is perfectly hard. Sometimes in warm weather the cake must stand overnight before the frosting is firm, but it is very rich looking when it finally hardens.

HICKORY NUT CAKE

Two cupfuls of sugar and one-half cupful of butter, creamed together. Add three egss and beat until creamed. One cupful of sweet milk, three cupfuls of sweet milk, three cupfuls of flour, two teaspoonfuls of baking powder and one cupful of nut meats. Bake in a steady oven.

Pancakes are used by Cather as a breakfast food (OO 6, 202) served with syrup, coffee, and sausages or bacon. I have never quite understood why she used the verb *to bake* with griddle cakes (OO 5, MA 354), since to me the use of a griddle suggests frying. The corn cakes described as a famine food served with sorghum molasses (MA 23) may have been either baked or fried. No waffles from an electric waffle iron have ever tasted as good as the ones from the black cast-iron waffle irons that fit directly over the top of a cookstove and can be flicked over with the turn of a wrist (MA 84).

The following recipes for breakfast cakes, griddle cakes, and waffles are from the Cathers' *Home Queen Cook Book* (pp. 286, 293):

Take 2 cups flour, ½ pt. sweet milk, a little salt, 2 eggs well beaten. Stir well. Bake in muffin-pans, in a quick oven.

Take 1 pt. milk, or ½ milk and water warmed, a little salt, ½ cup flour, 3 table-spoons yeast, 1 egg well beaten. Set to rise over night [*sic*]. Bake on hot gridiron, on both sides.

Take 1 cup sour milk, 2 table-spoons drawn butter, 2 eggs, a scant ½ tea-spoon soda, a little salt. Beat the eggs separately. Stir with flour into a thick batter. Bake in waffle-iron.

Six eggs beaten separately, 1 spoon butter and a little salt, yeast powder, 1 qt. flour, sweet milk to make rather thin batter.

In the pages of the Cathers' *White House Cook Book* we found the following handwritten recipe for Corn Meal Cakes:

One pint sour milk
Two eggs
Butter the size of a walnut melted
One teaspoon soda
Corn meal to make a batter
Baked in a hot oven

We found this recipe for corn cakes in an undated and untitled magazine clipping in the pages of the Cather family *Home Queen Cook Book*:

Mix one cupful of sifted bread flour, one-half cupful of yellow granulated corn meal, two level teaspoonfuls of baking-powder, one-half level teaspoonful of salt and one rounded tablespoonful of sugar; stir in one cupful of milk, one well-beaten egg and two tablespoonfuls of melted butter or lard. Beat it thoroughly and turn into greased muffin-pans and bake in a quick oven about twenty minutes.

Mush may seem to be a long way from pancakes and waffles, but as was mentioned earlier, it not only was served as a pudding-type food but also was let sit overnight so that it would "set up," in which case it could be fried in the morning and eaten with syrup or jelly like pancakes. In two passages in which mush is mentioned in Cather's plains pioneer works, it is seen as a soft cereal, in one case as a food for someone with bad teeth (oo 42) and in the other as a breakfast cereal (MA 124).

From Mrs. Lea's *Domestic Cookery* (pp. 78–79):

Mush will keep for several days in cool weather; the best way of making it is to have a pot of boiling water, and stir in corn meal, mixed with water, and salt enough to season the whole; let it boil, and if it is not thick enough you can add more meal; keep stirring all the time to prevent it from being lumpy. It should boil an hour.

To make cakes, take a quart of cold mush, mix in it half a pint of wheat flour, and a little butter or lard, make it out in little cakes with your hands; flour them and bake them on a griddle or in a dripping pan. Fried mush is a good plain dessert, eaten with sugar and cream. Cut the cold mush in slices, half an inch thick, or make them into small cakes, dip them in flour, and fry them in hot lard.

Finally, a breadstuff that was a popular European peasant food and a common plains pioneer food was dumplings. Dumplings permit the cook to prepare an entire meal, including soup or stew, in one container. Like pancakes, waffles, and fried bread, dumplings can be "baked" as a kind of bread without having to be placed in an oven.

Mary Cather Janney's Apple Dumplings:

2 c flour
1 tsp salt

3 tsp baking powder
1 T butter
¾ cup sweet milk
Mix dough lightly.
Roll in sheet and cover with diced apples. Roll like jelly roll and cut in 2" pieces. Lay in buttered pan. Cover with the following sauce:
1 c sugar
1 T flour
1 c water
Boil sauce and pour over dumplings
Bake in moderate oven.

From Adeline Spicka's recipe file we obtained the following typical recipe for Czech Potato Dumplings:

2 cups mashed potatoes freshly cooked or left over
About a half teas salt or less
1 egg beaten
1 cup flour
Stir & knead & shape into oblong pieces. Drop into rapidly boiling water. Cook for about 15 minutes or when knife comes out clean when cut in half to test.

And from the files of Virginia Hoffbauer:

1 egg
1 cup milk
1 teas salt
2 cups flour
4 teas Baking Powder
3 tabsp veg oil
Mix egg, milk, oil with 2 cup flour with Baking Powder. Add salt. Beat till mixed well then add ¾ cup flour. Then knead & roll into long roll. Cut 1 in. pieces, roll into bun, in thin oblong. Place on top of Sauer Kraut or Sweet Cabbage to steam. 10 to 15 min.

Along the same lines, but a combination of fried cakes and steamed or boiled dumplings, is this recipe for Mashed Potato Pancakes from Adeline Spicka:

2 cups left-over potatoes

1 cup flour
½ teas salt

Mix & knead on Bread Board. Shape into small balls. Roll thin about ¾ size of large skillet. Place on large plate divided by squares of waxed paper dusted with flour. Use flour also on Board for rolling out.

Fry on hot skillet with small amount of fat or oil for each cake. Done when large & small blisters appear. May be served for every meal. Like to put poppyseed filling (thinned down) & spread thinly over and roll up. Cut up and enjoy. Very old recipe from [my husband] Frank's mother.

As we smell Cather's kitchens, rich with dark brown breads, roasting meats, heavy stuffings, breakfasts of heavy waffles and muffins, there can be no doubt that we are dealing with the tables of farmers, men and women who eat not as an idle amusement but as a way of preparing for a hard day in the fields or the household.

But we can also sense that these foods are not without their pleasure. They are not just nourishment, they are yet another way of delighting in the harvest.

Vegetables, Fruit, Berries

The frontier diet was characterized by red meat. Beef animals were too valuable for casual slaughter by the sod–buster farmer and conditions were not good for the preservation of meat, but it was nothing like it had been in the Old Country, where beef was a rare commodity. Moreover, on the plains there was abundant game, and it was not reserved for the aristocratic rifle and table. It was perhaps the Great Plains region that established what is thought of today as the mainstream American diet.

The pioneer table was not dedicated solely to meat and bread however. There were vegetables and fruits, greens and berries. Not in the variety or of the sort that had been found in the markets and forests of Europe or east of the Appalachians, but gardens were a part of every homestead, in the country or in the village, and for the clever forager there were plums and berries, cress and greens aplenty, even on the plains grasslands.

By far and away the most common side-dish component mentioned by Cather is the potato. That is not surprising. The potato
had the advantage of bearing its fruit under the ground, away from
the grasshoppers and hail, grassfires and rabbits. Moreover, it
stored well if some care had been taken to dig a proper cellar. Here
we can note the neighbors' disapproval of the sad situation of the
Shimerdas in *My Ántonia,* with only a few rotting and frozen potatoes in a barrel, potatoes gathered from the garbage. While the
Burdens gave the Czech family another sack of potatoes, the first
question Grandmother Burden asked was, "This is no place to keep
vegetables. How did your potatoes get frozen?" (MA 74)

A bag of potatoes constituted a generous gift of survival and
might spell the difference between joy and despair, even life and
death (MA 17). I like to think that one of the joys of potatoes is that
the treasure is not like that of an apple tree or tomato plant that you
watch develop during the summer. You count the tomatoes as they
grow and you have a pretty good idea of how they are coming along
and what you can anticipate on the table.

The humble potato carries with it the wonderful joy of buried
treasure. One moment there is only a withered, ugly bush, dying
before the approach of fall. And then as the tines of the pitchfork
rake up through the soil, there is a tumble of brown or red nuggets,
seeing the light of day for the first time. An apple tree has all its
prizes before you and you can calculate as you pick how many more
baskets you will need. But the potato surprises you every time, and
there seems to be more need for haste, as if to grab them before they
disappear back into the ground. You rake your fingers through the
soil and find even those fruits that are hidden, and I have noticed a
tendency to try to carry all the potatoes from one bush in one
armload, so that there seems always to be a superabundance, more
than one can carry at one time (MA 16).

Another advantage of the humble potato is the ease of its preparation. The mystery of the potato for me has been how little is
made of it as a raw foodstuff. My mother and my wife have always
had trouble getting peeled potatoes to the pot because I would just as
soon eat them raw, with a dash of salt. Cather does not provide

specific information about the way she imagines or experienced potatoes being prepared for the pioneer table, but perhaps the subtle hints she gives us are enough. A passage from *O Pioneers!* (p. 85), for example, suggests that they were served whole, boiled or baked:

The three pretty young Swedish girls who did Alexandra's homework were cutting pies, refilling coffee-cups, placing platters of bread and meat and potatoes upon the red tablecloth. . . .

As does another passage earlier:

Lou reached for a potato. (OP 57)

There is a potato passage which is one of the most subtle of Cather's works. I am never quite sure whether the intention is truly Cather's or is only a matter of my imposing my own judgments on a harmless statement. But I think I know Cather and Mahailey and Enid and myself well enough to sort it out correctly. The passage is in *One of Ours* (p. 195). Mahailey is generally troubled by the fact that Claude Wheeler's vegetarian and otherwise "progressive" wife has apparently abandoned him. She herself is possessive and ferociously maternal, resenting anything that smacks of abandonment:

If one of the Yoeder boys or Susie Dawson happened to be at the Wheelers' for dinner, Mahailey never failed to refer to Enid in a loud voice. "Mr. Claude's wife, she cuts her potatoes up raw in the pan an' fries 'em. She don't boil 'em first like I do. I know she's an awful good cook, I know she is." She felt that easy references to the absent wife made things look better.

It may be an easy reference and it may have been done to make things look better, but we do not believe that it was done to make Enid look better, only Claude. Mahailey thinks Enid is a terrible cook, especially since she is a vegetarian. She simply doesn't take the time and care to boil her potatoes before she fries them. She just cuts them right into the pan. But I'm sure she's a good cook. I mean, I'm really sure she is a good cook, no matter what everyone else says. We may surmise from the passage that Mahailey does boil her potatoes before she fries them and that she knows as well as everyone else that

that is the proper way to do it. And we think it is too. Moreover, they should be fried in real lard, or butter, with bits of bacon sliced in, or with greens.

Likewise we may surmise, somewhat to our surprise, that potatoes were not served in Cather's pioneer country in the form of dumplings. In *One of Ours* (p. 73) Cather writes:

If Mrs. Erlich and her Hungarian woman made lentil soup and potato dumplings and Wiener-Schnitzel for him, it only made the plain fare on the farm seem the heavier.

We have always felt that the difference between rural and urban fare, so vividly described throughout *One of Ours,* is one of function. A different sort of table is set for the farm boy, who is working in the wind and cold of a Nebraska field all day, than is set before the university student, who will spend the day sitting at a desk in a heated room. Dumplings are rural pioneer peasant fare too, and we are not certain of the suggestion that they are an urban high-style dish. At any rate the dumpling recipes provided in the previous chapter will allow the reader to decide for himself the relative displacement factors.

We do not find mention in Cather of sweet potatoes' being served but they were, for we do find them as part of the inventory of the pioneer garden:

One September afternoon Alexandra had gone over to the garden across the draw to dig sweet potatoes—they had been thriving upon the weather that was fatal to everything else. (OP 48)

From a newspaper clipping, untitled but dated January 26, 1910, found between the pages of the Cathers' *White House Cook Book*:

Parboil the potatoes, and slice while hot. Butter a deep dish, put in a layer of potatoes, sprinkle with sugar, salt, pepper and dots of butter, then a stratum of fine crumbs, and well buttered. Pour in four tablespoonfuls of warm water to generate steam, cover closely and bake half an hour. Uncover and brown. This is especially nice for a family dinner and approved by children.

From the *White House Cook Book* (p. 186):

The potatoes should be boiled whole with the skins on in plenty of water, well salted, and are much better for being boiled the day before needed. Care should be taken that they are not over-cooked. Strip off the skins (not pare them with a knife) and slice them nearly a quarter of an inch thick. Place them in a chopping bowl and sprinkle over them sufficient salt and pepper to season them well; chop them all one way, then turn the chopping bowl half way around, and chop across them, cutting them into little square pieces the shape of dice. About twenty-five minutes before serving time, place on the stove a saucepan (or any suitable dish) containing a piece of butter the size of an egg; when it begins to melt and run over the bottom of the dish, put in a cup of rich sweet milk. When this boils up put in the chopped potatoes; there should be about a quart of them; stir them a little so that they become moistened through with the milk; then cover and place them on the back of the stove, or in a moderate oven, where they will heat through gradually. When heated through, stir carefully from the bottom with a spoon and cover tightly again. Keep hot until ready to serve. Baked potatoes are very good warmed in this manner.

Recipes frequently call for potato water. The water that potatoes have been boiled in is used by *great* cooks for gravies and soups.

We were uncertain about the propriety of associating squashes with potatoes, but our reasoning was that they seem to fall into roughly the same sort of dish category at a meal, even though they do not grow the same in the garden. Our concerns were put to rest when we began to look more closely at Cather's treatment of the two, for in case after case she puts the two together, in the same paragraph, in the same sentence:

We found Russian Peter digging his potatoes. We were glad to go in and get warm by his kitchen stove and to see his squashes and Christmas melons, heaped in the storeroom for winter. (MA 43–44)

Squash, pumpkins, and potatoes are all New World products and therefore were well suited to the conditions of the plains. They stored well and provided large fruits. They were popular in the pioneer garden and on the pioneer table.

Pumpkins and squash were served as a hot vegetable as well as in pies, and potatoes (especially sweet potatoes) were served both in pies and as vegetables. Cather notes in *My Ántonia* (p. 19) that a suitable gift for hungry neighbors was a pumpkin pie—and a sack of potatoes.

The following recipe for pumpkin as a vegetable is in the Czech style and comes from the recipe file of Alice Styskal:

Wash the pumpkin well, peel it and take out all the seeds. Cut in strips or cubes and dust with a little salt and let stand for at least fifteen minutes. Drain and dry with clean cloth, dip in flour and fry in hot lard. To serve, arrange on hot dish and dust with a little salt and pepper.

The only pumpkin recipes in the Cather files are for pumpkin pie, the first from *The Home Queen Cook Book* (p. 393), where it is circled and underlined, and the second from a handwritten note found between the pages of *The White House Cook Book*:

One qt. pumpkin stewed well, 4 eggs, 1 cup cream or sweet milk, sugar to taste (about 2 cups sugar), 2 or 3 large spoons brandy, ½ nutmeg; bake with rather a short crust in quick oven.

¾ cup white sugar
½ cup milk
2 eggs
3 spoons sliced pumpkins
Mix well. sugar-yolks of eggs & pumpkin
Then the whites beaten stiff. lastly milk—flavor with cinnamon, ginger and nutmeg. (When eggs are scarce use a little flour.)

Cather uses pumpkins and squash not only as food but also as a part of the home context, certainly in part because they are such colorful fruits:

Ducks and geese ran quacking across my path. White cats were sunning themselves among the yellow pumpkins on the porch steps. (MA 330)

One of the most charming descriptions of the pumpkin in Cather's work is not as a foodstuff but as a backrest:

I sat down in the middle of the garden, where snakes could scarcely approach unseen, and leaned my back against a warm yellow pumpkin. (MA 17–18)

If potatoes are the mystery plant of the garden, hidden away totally, then squash are the most flamboyant producers. They are huge, frequently vividly colorful, and as everything else of the garden withers away in the late summer and early fall, there they are, seeming to grow all the larger as their umbilical cords fall away. Perhaps that is why Cather so often describes squash not on the table but in the garden:

Alone, I should never have found the garden—except, perhaps, for the big yellow pumpkins that lay about unprotected by their withering vines. . . . (MA 16)

This discussion of squash may be the appropriate place to say something in general about the pioneer garden according to Cather. Peter and Pavel, the Russians, have melons, squashes, and cucumbers in their garden (MA 35), and Mrs. Voigt, the German cook in Lincoln, grew peas (OO 210–11). Jim Burden and Ántonia went to gather vegetables from the Burden family garden early in the morning, while the dew was still on the grass (MA 138).

Alexandra is described in *O Pioneers!* as looking like the double sunflowers that fringed her garden (p. 88) and unlike the women of her time who prized translucent white skin: "Her face is always tanned in summer, for her sunbonnet is oftener on her arm than on her head" (OP 88). Perhaps that was also in part a result of her use of her garden not only as a source of food but also as a place for quiet contemplation:

. . . when Carl Linstrum came up the garden rows to find her, she was not working. She was standing lost in thought, leaning upon her pitchfork, her sunbonnet lying beside her on the ground. The dry garden patch smelled of drying vines and was strewn with yellow seed-cucumbers and pumpkins and citrons. At one end, next the rhubarb, grew feathery asparagus, with red berries. Down the middle of the garden was a row of gooseberry and currant bushes. A few tough zenias and marigolds and a row of scarlet sage bore witness to the buckets of water that Mrs. Bergson had carried there after sundown. . . . (OP 48–49)

Today when we so casually turn a faucet handle to get water to our lawns or gardens, we forget the incredible effort it took a pioneer woman to water her garden. Her plot was likely to be a quarter-acre, perhaps more, and whatever water was led to it was probably brought by bucketfuls, one by one. Potato bugs were picked off the plants one by one, and cultivating was done with a hoe.

But a garden was not just an amusement, a gesture, an excuse to be outdoors. It was part and parcel of the family's survival and so it was not rare that the man of the family would help with a garden just as the woman of the family knew that her work might be necessary to bring in the crops:

[Claude] watered the gourd vine before he went to milk. It was not really a gourd vine at all, but a summer-squash, of the crook-necked, warty, orange-coloured variety, and it was now full of ripe squashes, hanging by strong stems among the rough green leaves and prickly tendrils. Claude had watched its rapid growth and the opening of its splotchy yellow blossoms, feeling grateful to a thing that did so lustily what is was put there to do. (OO 177)

Just as water was a luxury for the pioneer garden, so too were such things as pesticides. I have often read that earlier garden passage and wondered whether Cather was telling us about pioneer methods of insect control. Flowers like zinnias and marigolds often were planted around or within a vegetable garden for their virtue as insect and weed repellents.

One of the primal joys of my life is asparagus. Asparagus grows at almost precisely the same time that the morel mushroom appears along plains rivers, so a canoe trip at that time (variously predicted as the last weekend in April, the day the lilacs bloom, and when an oak tree's leaves are the size of a squirrel's ear) is a gourmet's delight. But, as is the case with potatoes, I have never been able to get wild asparagus into a steamer because it is so impossibly succulent and delicious raw.

I was once hunting wild asparagus along the banks of the Middle Loup near our farm at Dannebrog and found a nice patch of short, thick stalks stabbing up from the ground. I picked a couple and ate them, only moments from their stalks, and great beads of juice dropped off the bottoms of the picked stalks. If asparagus fresh is a thousand times better than asparagus canned, and if asparagus picked and eaten in moments is better by a thousand times than asparagus picked and sent to market days later, what would asparagus eaten directly from the stalk be like? I was concerned—very concerned—with what a passing fisherman or hunter might think should he see me, but I got down on my hands and knees and bit asparagus directly from the stalk. My mouth waters at this very moment at the thought of that ambrosial grazing.

If you can bear to bring asparagus to heat before you eat it, steam it rather than cook it. And take Cather's hint: find it when its tall, feathery fronds and red berries signal its camp, then return in the spring when the spears first thrust up from the warming mold.

The Cather files contain no asparagus recipes that can be identified as family favorites, but Alice Styskal has provided us with three representative recipes from pioneer Nebraska kitchens. We might note that for our own tastes we prefer to steam asparagus:

Wash asparagus and cut away the hard ends making stalks all the same length. Make a bundle with all the tips together and tie with a strong thread. Boil in salted water careful not to overboil as the tips will break. Then drain, take off the thread and arrange on a warm platter and sprinkle with buttered bread crumbs.

Boil as shown in the preceding recipe. Arrange on a dish and serve with gravy made as follows. Cream two tablespoons of butter, add four egg yolks and cream again, then add a tablespoon of flour, the juice of a lemon, a pinch of salt and cream again. Then add two cups of good soup or hot water, and stir until it thickens.

Wash and cut asparagus into pieces about an inch long. Boil in salted water. In a skillet, blend a little butter and flour together but do not brown. Add some soup to make gravy, then add to this some fresh sliced mushrooms and simmer a bit. Arrange the asparagus on a dish and pour the gravy over it and serve.

Cather's gardens contained tomatoes (OP 29), sweet corn (OO 175), beans, and cucumbers (MA 36). Most garden produce could be eaten fresh, and I will deal with these recipes here, but most important they could also be preserved for the hard plains winters, and I will treat the topic of food preservation a bit later.

Cather herself comments on a recipe for cucumbers; here we see her as the observer of a culture of which she was a part, the early plains, but one made up of many alien components. Thus while she knew the plains as well as anyone, she still might find new ideas and new foods. Here it is the Russians who suggest a new idea for a common garden vegetable:

Before we left, Peter put ripe cucumbers into a sack for Mrs. Shimerda and gave us a lard-pail full of milk to cook them in. I had never heard of cooking cucumbers, but Ántonia assured me they were very good. (MA 37)

Linda's Czech family knows well what Ántonia was speaking of. Here is their own recipe from Linda's file:

Make sure the cukes are not bitter. Peel and slice them into a bowl. Salt them and let them stand an hour or more. Drain the liquid. Pepper and add vinegar. Stir in some heavy cream and mix to coat the cukes. Keep cool until ready to eat.

From the Cathers' *White House Cook Book* (p. 167):

Peel and slice twelve good, sound, fresh tomatoes; the slices about a quarter of an inch thick. Set them on the ice or in a refrigerator while you make the dressing. . . . Take one head of the broad-leaved variety of lettuce, wash, and arrange them neatly around the sides of the bowl. Place the cold, sliced tomatoes in the centre. Pour over the dressing and serve.

From the same source, page 168:

Put into two quarts of tomato pulp (or two cans of canned tomatoes) one onion, cut fine, two tablespoons of salt and three tablespoons of brown sugar. Boil until quite thick; then take from the fire and strain it through a sieve, working it until it is all through but the seeds. Put it back on the stove, and add two tablespoonfuls of ground cloves, half a teaspoonful of cayenne pepper, one grated nutmeg, one pint of good vinegar; boil it until it will just run from the mouth of a bottle. It should be watched, stirred often, that it does not burn. If sealed tight while hot, in large-mouthed bottles, it will keep good for years.

From Mrs. Lea's *Domestic Cookery* (p. 165):

Scald and peel a peck of ripe tomatoes; cut them in slices and lay them on a large dish; cover well with salt each layer; the next morning put the tomatoes in a colander or on a sifter, and drain off all the liquid; then mash them with a wooden masher, and to each quart, put a pint of strong vinegar, two table-spoonsful of white mustard seed, a dozen cloves, a dozen grains of black pepper, an onion sliced and chopped, a tablespoonful of salt; if mashed fine you can pour it out of wide-mouthed bottles; put a tablespoonful of spirits in each bottle at the top; cork tight, and seal. If you prefer putting the sauce in small stone jars, put spirits on paper at the top of each.

The following recipe for tomato preserves, torn from page 9 of the September, 1909, issue of *Woman's World,* was placed between the pages of the Cathers' *White House Cook Book*:

Use the small yellow tomatoes, perfectly ripe and sound. Pour boiling water over them and peel, being careful to keep them whole. Weigh the tomatoes and allow an equal quantity of sugar; to each pound of sugar use half a lemon, sliced thin with the seeds removed. Put the sugar and lemons in the preserving kettle with just enough water to moisten the sugar and heat slowly until it dissolves. Boil and skim until clear, then put in the tomatoes and boil gently for three-quarters of an hour. Cool and place in jars.

We will be dealing with pickles later, but it seems appropriate to include at this point a recipe for Green Tomato Pickles from the files of Alice Styskal:

Take an enameled pot, put in one gallon of sliced green tomatoes, two quarts of vinegar, one quart of sugar, a fourth cup of mustard seed, two teaspoons of whole allspice and one teaspoon of ground pepper, one tablespoon of salt and a dozen sliced onions. Cook this for ten minutes. Then put it in a stone jar and cover and keep in a cool place.

Darlene Divis provided us with this traditional recipe for green beans:

Brown onion in little oil. Drain. Add 1–2 pints stewed tomatoes, 1 tsp brown sugar, salt, pepper, 1 tsp wochester [*sic*] sauce, ¼ cup catsup. Heat and thicken with 2 heaping spoons corn-starch mixed in water (little). Add to 1–2 pints green beans and rest of stuff. Boil till thickened.

The following recipe for ten-minute canned beans was shared with us by Debbie Novacek of Seward:

Prepare beans as for cold packing (clean & rinse & remove ends). Bring to a boil 1 gal. water, ½ cup canning salt, ½ cup vinegar. Put as many beans in this as it will take care of & boil 10 minutes vigorously. Place in sterilized jars & seal while hot. When you use them, pour liquid off & put clear water on them & they taste like fresh. Very good recipe.

This recipe for canned pork and beans is from the pioneer kitchen of Grandma Emily Kresse of Brainard:

Soak navy beans overnight, sterilize jars, cut up pork and put it in the bottom of the jars. Fill with the beans until ¾ full. Add mixture of ketchup, brown sugar, pepper and salt diluted with water. Screw lids lightly. Cook two hours in a canner cooker, very slowly. Then screw lids tightly shut, let cool, then store.

All of the following recipes for corn were found in an undated newspaper clipping, titled "Some Ways of Preparing and Serving the Typical American Dish," inserted between the pages of the Cathers' *White House Cook Book*:

Select Evergreen corn, white as snow, plump bodied, with tender green husks, slender stalk and dark brown silk. Strip down the husks and test its freshness by pressing the thumb nail in one or two of the kernels. If the milk flows freely the corn is in the pink of condition. Strip off the outer husks leaving the tender inside ones on, but turning them back. Remove every thread of silk, rubbing it off with the hands. Now turn the inner husks back, tie with an outside husk and place in a kettle. Cover the corn over with a layer of the outside husks, then pour on cold water to the depth of the corn, put on the kettle lid and set over a quick fire. Watch carefully and after the water has boiled just five minutes from the time it reaches the boiling point, it is done. Serve at once, leaving the inside husks on, or not as preferred. The ears should be folded in a serviette when sent to the table.

Boiling water may be used in place of the cold and the corn boiled exactly eight minutes from the time the boiling point is reached; but it will not be quite so delicious as with the cold water process. The great difficulty with many cooks is that they overcook corn and corn cooked too long toughens.

Another nice way to cook tender corn is in milk. In this case husk the corn and drop into the boiling milk. Cook just five minutes from the time it begins to boil. Keep covered closely while cooking, and serve as soon as done. Where there is a large family to be provided with corn it is wiser to cook the corn in relays.

[Indian corn pudding] is one of the gastronomic delights of midsummer. Select firm, fresh ears of corn, medium size, and with a keen bladed knife score each row of kernels, then scrape out the pulp, leaving the hulls on the cob. To the pulp taken from a dozen ears allow a pint and a half rich milk, four beaten eggs, a teaspoonful salt, a half teaspoonful pepper, and if the corn lacks sweetness, two or three tablespoonfuls sugar. Bake in a well buttered deep earthen dish for two hours, in a slow, steady oven.

[For corn fritters] cut the kernels from four good sized ears young corn. Add two beaten eggs, half a teaspoonful salt, a salt spoonful pepper, a cup of flour pressed down and heaped a little, and a cup cold milk. Have ready a hot frying pan well greased and drop in the batter by spoonfuls. There should be enough for a dozen. Do not let the fritters touch. Cook in relays, frying on one side four minutes, then turn and fry on the other. These are delicious as an accompaniment for chicken or to serve for breakfast.

Peabody Hale of Crawford, a noted pioneer musician and certifiable character, told me that to this day he cannot judge the ripeness of a watermelon unless he buys it at night. He told me that when he was a youngster he once crawled hundreds of yards through a field to reach a secret watermelon patch. Just as he reached it, he heard a shout and a shot, so he grabbed the biggest melon he could and stuffed it into the front of his bib overalls. He struggled back on hands and knees, pursued by occasional shots and the rake of buckshot through the dry cornstalks above his head. He said he has never experienced a greater disappointment than he felt on that occasion when he discovered that he had brought back a pumpkin instead of a watermelon.

Cather's gardens have watermelon patches, and pioneer accounts mention melons again and again. They were sweet, and sweetness was at a premium in those days. They were full of juice, and juices on the plains were at a premium too. Chilled in a horse tank or a river channel, a melon was the closest thing to refrigerated soft drinks a pioneer might experience. Stolen, a melon could reach dimensions of lusciousness that are utterly indescribable.

One grower told me he always figured that kids would steal about a quarter of his crop and that was fine with him. But when he heard the dogs barking and saw that they sensed something going on in the field, he said, he would fire a couple of shotgun blasts over the field just to add that special savor. "Nothing flavors melons," he said, "like gunpowder."

Like asparagus, melons are best eaten as fresh as possible:

When the lesson was over, we used to go up to the watermelon patch behind the garden. I split the melons with an old corn-knife, and we lifted out the hearts and ate them with the juice trickling through our fingers. The white Christmas melons we did not touch, but we watched them with curiosity. They were to be picked late, when the hard frosts had set in, and put away for winter use. (MA 30–31)

One of the happiest scenes in *My Ántonia* is an orgy of watermelon eating at which Russian Peter is host:

After he had shown us his garden, Peter trundled a load of watermelons up the hill in his wheelbarrow. . . .

Peter put the melons in a row on the oilcloth-covered table and stood over them, brandishing a butcher knife. Before the blade got fairly into them, they split of their own ripeness, with a delicious sound. He gave us knives, but no plates, and the top of the table was soon swimming with juice and seeds. I had never seen anyone eat so many melons as Peter ate. He assured us that they were good for one—better than medicine; in his country people lived on them at this time of the year. (MA 36–37)

Therefore it is perhaps one of the saddest events in Cather's pioneer works when Peter and Pavel lose their farm and, like so many plains people of the past and the present, must see it dismantled and sold piece by piece to the highest bidder, one of the cruelest features of American culture:

At his sale we bought Peter's wheelbarrow and some of his harness. During the auction he went about with his head down, and never lifted his eyes. He seemed not to care about anything. The Black Hawk money-lender who held mortgages on Peter's livestock was there, and he bought in the sale notes at about fifty cents on the dollar. Everyone said Peter kissed the cow before she was led away by her new owner. I did not see him do it, but this I know: after all his furniture and his cook-stove and pots and pans had been hauled off by the purchasers, when his house was stripped and bare, he sat down on the floor with his clasp-knife and ate all the melons that he had put away for winter. When Mr. Shimerda and Krajiek drove up in their wagon to take Peter to the train, they found him with a dripping beard, surrounded by heaps of melon rinds. (MA 60–61)

The following three recipes—Citron Preserves, Pie Melon Pie, and Watermelon Preserves—are from Mrs. Berniece Pelt of Stockton, Kansas, who taught in Red Cloud fourteen years:

Remove rind from citron melon. Cut inner rind into 1 inch squares. Cover with warm water and cook slowly until tender. Drain. To each pound of melon rind add
½ cup raisins
½ lemon sliced
2 cups sugar
1 teaspoon whole cloves
1 stick cinnamon
1 cup hot water
Simmer slowly, stirring frequently, until thick. Mother put the spices in a thin cloth bag and removed them. (Square of cheesecloth tied with string.)

Use your best apple pie recipe. Add 2 tablespoons lemon juice to the filling. it is 75 years since I have heard of pie melons. Green melons, green to the center.

Cut a melon rind into 1 inch strips. Pare away the hard surface and all the pink meat except a very thin layer. Cover with brine (1 Tbsp salt to 1 qt water). Let stand over night. Drain. Dice. Measure the fruit into a large kettle and add 1 thinly sliced lemon, 2 tsp cinnamon, ¼ tsp ginger to 6 to 8 pints of fruit. Place over the fire and simmer until fruit is clear and tender. The syrup will be thick like honey when dripped on a cold dish.

The following recipe for Watermelon Rind Preserves was torn from page 9 of the September, 1909, issue of *Woman's World* and inserted between the pages of the Cathers' *White House Cook Book*:

After the rind is peeled, weigh it; to each pound allow a pound of sugar, an ounce of green ginger root, a lemon and a half a pint of water. Scrape the ginger root and tie it in a clean cloth, with the yellow rind of the lemon, pared very thin; squeeze the juice of the lemon and strain it. Put the sugar and water over the fire and let them heat together and begin to boil, removing all the scum as it rises; when the syrup is free from scum put in the watermelon rind, ginger, lemon peel and juice and boil all together until the rind looks clear, removing any scum which may rise. Let the preserve cool in the kettle, put into glass jars, leaving the ginger and lemon with it if their flavor is desired, and distributing them among the jars.

Although the settlers did not generally adopt Indian food-ways, they did bring with them some of their own traditional uses of wild food plants. There were of course no supermarkets on the frontier with cooled counters of fresh lettuce, cabbage, or spinach, so the pioneer housewife used the cheaper, more convenient, and more healthful system of stepping outside her sod-house door and picking wild greens as they came into season.

Charley O'Kieffe writes in *Western Story*:

During the summer months weeds contributed much to our table. As in most countries, weeds—vegetables out of place, as some people call them—grew in profusion, creating lots of problems and entailing lots of work in their eradication or control. But in the O'Kieffe home our slogan was, "If you can't beat 'em, eat 'em." The names of three of these helpful little pests come to mind as I write: pigweed, lambsquarter, and pussley [purslane]. . . . Mother had a way of slipping a small hunk of salt pork in the pot with the cooking weeds and, brother, that made the difference.

O'Kieffe's mother knew her stuff. She picked three of the choicest of weed greens to feed her family. And they are as good today as they were then. Perhaps the most important addition I could make to her list is dandelions, and Cather's character Mahailey knew about that delight, as we shall learn later.

Salads are not pioneer food. A friend of mine, of pioneer ranch stock, once pronounced that he simply "don't put green things in his mouth." The unattractive Enid is a vegetarian. Unlike Ántonia's warm, cluttered, happy kitchen with its hot, rich, buttered, seasoned, heavy foods, Enid's kitchen is

full of the afternoon sun, glittered with new paint, spotless linoleum, and blue-and-white cooking vessels. In the dining-room the cloth was laid, and the table was neatly set for one. Claude opened the icebox, where his supper was arranged for him; a dish of canned salmon with a white sauce; hardboiled eggs, peeled and lying in a nest of lettuce leaves; a bowl of ripe tomatoes, a bit of cold rice pudding; cream and butter. (OO 173)

This is how a woman cooks who has no warmth and love of her own. Salads!

Mahailey makes salads too, but she is full of love and concern and she explicitly sees her food as an expression of that love. How, then, can she reconcile salads to a regimen of love and concern? She does not use lettuce, that green so alien to the plains, especially when it has been robbed of its very life strength by being grown under shade so that it is more white than green. No, Mahailey gathers greens, the wild salads that the gods provide, out of the same warmth and love with which she conveys them to the table. Her method, interpreted by some as a sign of her madness, is not her own idiosyncratic interpretation:

Along the roadsides, from under the dead weeds and wisps of dried bluestem, the dandelions thrust up their clean, bright faces. If Claude happened to step on one, the acrid smell made him think of Mahailey, who had probably been out this very morning, gouging the sod with her broken butcher-knife and stuffing dandelion greens into her apron. She always went for greens with an air of secrecy, very early, and sneaked along the roadsides stooping close to the ground, as if she might be detected and driven away, or as if the dandelions were wild things and had to be caught sleeping. (OO 105–6)

Precisely! It is a widespread belief among peoples of many societies that greens and some berries (chokecherries, for example) must indeed by snuck up on early in the morning or they will taste bitter. Mahailey was not at all crazy: she was merely following the prescribed method for producing the best meal for the family she loved. Mahailey's greens, we may surmise, were never bitter.

Nothing provides a better soapbox for a discussion of pioneer foodways and their quality than that passage. I suspect there are those who will cluck their tongues at the prospect of having to gather wild leaves for a supper salad. How fortunate we are today to have our lettuce. I recall the time I didn't have time to gather wild greens for a salad and my son Chris came to the supper table, looked at the lettuce salad with some dismay, and said, "What's the matter, Dad, are we out of weeds?"

Dandelions gathered before they blossom (and turn bitter) are a delight. As are the other greens Mahailey most assuredly gathered: lambsquarter, plantain, dock, purslane. They are cheap (that is to say, free), infinitely more convenient and nutritious than store-bought greens, tastier, and easier to prepare.

Mahailey gathered her dandelions with a knife because she was also gathering the crown, the succulent white segment between the leaves and the root. The leaves could be served as a salad green or a cooked green (cook them only a minute or two), the crowns could be steamed as a vegetable, and perhaps she was even harvesting some of the roots to be roasted to the state of fuming (black and crisp through and through) to be added as a stretcher to the coffee supply. (When you roast dandelion roots you should be prepared to have all the neighbors call you to tell you that your chocolate cake is burning. That is precisely what it smells like, and the addition of dandelion gives coffee a charmingly mellow mocha taste.)

There is always concern about accidentally including poisonous plants with non-toxic foods, and there should be. There are dangerous and poisonous plants growing in the wild. But then there are poisonous plants in the garden (rhubarb leaves and roots, for example) and all manner of poisonous substances on grocery store shelves (lye, roach poison, and American processed cheeses, for example), but we learn quickly and easily how to deal with those choices. It doesn't take much more effort than that to learn about the bounty of the countryside. For Mahailey, such knowledge was a part of her everyday life, just as unself-conscious an activity as picking up a bag of potato chips in the supermarket might be for us.

There is indication that Cather's people recognized watercress (OO 131), and it seems likely that they would have made use of this splendid seasoning in their salads and soups. Watercress likes clean, running water, so it has suffered severely from the abuse we have dealt out to our rivers in the intervening century, but I have found watercress along some of the side streams of the Niobrara, the Calumus, and even the North and Middle Loup rivers in Nebraska. It was found along the Niobrara until a few years ago, when bizarre irregularities in water level and sand burdens were induced, perhaps to frustrate canoers, who are often opponents of the destruction of that magnificent piece of water. The Republican River may have been a source of cress for Red Cloud families in Cather's day.

An abundant and pleasant substitute for cress from our gardens is the nasturtium (Latin for "nose twister"), which tastes like a slightly coarse cress but which can grace a salad or soup.

The following commentary for peppergrass and cress, common plains weeds, is from page 168 of the Cather family's *White House Cook Book*:

These are used mostly as an appetizer, served simply with salt. Cresses are occasionally used in making salads.

A handwritten note in the pages of the Cathers' *Home Queen Cook Book* carried a recipe labeled, simply, "salad dressing":

Yolk 3 eggs—well beaten
5 tablespoons vinegar
Handfull sugar
Lump butter—cook till it thickens then thin with cream, apples & celery—half & half.

Mrs. Berniece Pelt, who spent many years in Willa Cather's Red Cloud, offered this as a typical salad dressing of the area:

½ cup vinegar
½ cup water
Butter the size of a walnut
3 egg yolks
1 large tbsp sugar
½ tbsp flour
½ tsp salt
¼ tsp mustard
Pepper

Hold back the eggs until you have cooked the other ingredients until it thickens. Add a little of the hot mixture to the beaten eggs. Beat then add to the hot mixture and cook a few more seconds. (Keeps the eggs from lumping.)

Helen Obitz helped us with the following recipe for boiled salad dressing from Grace Frisbie Frame:

(Very good for potato salad)
1 c vinegar
1 c water
1½ c sugar
2 t dry mustard
1 t salt
1 T flour
2 eggs
2 T butter

Combine dry ingredients. Add eggs, vinegar and water. Boil until thick. Add butter. Makes 2 pts.

For reasons that are not clear to me, soup has come to be closely associated with salads in our society, perhaps because they both smack of health. Soups are not explicitly used as literary devices by Cather, but they are so much of the plains rural peasant diet that they can scarely go unmentioned in this examination. A handwritten note inserted in the Cathers' copy of *The White House Cook Book* offers a recipe for vegetable soup:

Scald, peel & mash 1 pk ripe tomatoes
Run through the grinder
2 head cabbage

1 doz. Medium size carrot

1 bunch parsley

½ pk onions / 3 stalks celery

Boil 1 doz. ears corn on the cob for 10 min., cut off and scrape. Mix all together & add a small handful of salt to every gallon. If mixture seems dry, add water, boil until carrots are thoroughly cooked. Seal while hot in qt. jars.

In winter add contents of jar to soup stock. This makes 11 qts.

A Cather family lentil soup recipe was provided to us by Mary Lambrecht of Red Cloud:

1 cup chopped onions

4 tsp bacon drippings

1 cup dried lentils

1 clove garlic, pressed (optional)

2 tsp salt

1 tsp freshly-ground pepper

2 smoked pork shanks or 1 ham bone

1 bay leaf

2 whole cloves

1 ½ cup sliced carrots

2 qts cold water

2 cups cubed red potatoes

In dutch oven saute onions in bacon drippings until glossy. Add lentils, garlic, salt and pepper; stir until onion turns yellow and lentils begin to make a noise. Add pork shanks, bay leaf, cloves tied in cheesecloth, and the carrots. Add the water and bring to a gentle boil. Cover; simmer about 30 minutes. Add potatoes and cook 1 ½ hours. Before serving, remove cheesecloth and pass soup through food mill, strain, add 1 cup of thin cream or half-half, or yogurt. Can be garnished with frankfurters or croutettes. (Cheese croutettes are very good.) Split peas can be used in place of lentils.

Soups were popular on the pioneer plains because they were hot and nourishing, could include almost anything, and because they could be easily divided among any number of family members and guests.

These two popular recipes for soups are from *A Treasury of Nebraska Pioneer Folkore* (p. 322):

CORN SOUP

One pint each of corn, boiling water, and milk, one slice of onion, two tablespoons of butter, two tablespoons of flour, one teaspoon of salt, a few grains of pepper. Chop the corn, add the water, and simmer for twenty minutes; run the mixture through a sieve. Scald the milk with the onion and add the milk to the corn. Thicken with mixture of butter and flour. Add salt and pepper.

PRINCE WILLIAM SOUP

Cook slowly, in enough water to cover, a mixture of dried fruits such as apricots, prunes, pears, raisins, and currants. Add a little soaked tapioca to thicken and cook slowly until done.

Today we can buy apples, pears, or oranges at almost any time of the year. They are brought to the Great Plains from Florida, California, and even Israel. It was not so easy during pioneer years, and the time required for the delivery of fruit might not be measured so much in days as in decades:

Marie came back with a branch she had broken from an apricot tree, laden with pale-yellow, pink-cheeked fruit. She dropped it beside Carl. "Did you plant those, too? They are such beautiful little trees."

Carl fingered the blue-green leaves, porous like blotting paper and shaped like birch leaves, hung on waxen red stems. "Yes, I think I did. Are these the circus trees, Alexandra?"

"Shall I tell her about them?" Alexandra asked. "Sit down like a good girl, Marie, and don't ruin my poor hat, and I'll tell you a story. A long time ago, when Carl and I were, say, sixteen and twelve, a circus came to Hanover and we went to town in our wagon, with Lou and Oscar, to see the parade. We had n't money enough to go to the circus. We followed the parade out to the circus grounds and hung around until the show began and the crowd went inside the tent. Then Lou was afraid we looked foolish standing outside in the pasture, so we went back to Hanover feeling very sad. There was a man in the streets selling apricots, and we had never seen any before. He had driven down from somewhere up in the French country, and he was selling them twenty-five cents a peck. We had a little money our fathers had given us for candy, and I bought two pecks and Carl bought one. They cheered us a good deal, and we saved all the seeds and planted them. Up to the time Carl went away, they had n't borne at all."

"And now he's come back to eat them," cried Marie, nodding at Carl. (OP 136–38)

More likely sources of fruit were the hollows and creek banks, where wild plums, fox grapes, and chokecherries could always be found in season, if the hopeful hunter could beat the birds to the harvest.

Cather is one of the few observers of the plains to remark on the ground-cherry. Few plainsmen today know the plant, except perhaps as children, when the Chinese-lantern fruit is called pop berries because the paper-covered fruit can be popped between the hands. In *My Ántonia,* Jim Burden enjoys them fresh from the bush:

There were some ground-cherry bushes growing along the furrows, full of fruit. I turned back the papery triangular sheaths that protected the berries and ate a few. (MA 18)

The Shimerdas, newly arrived from the long trial of the ocean crossing, hungered for the taste of fresh fruit:

The two girls would wander for miles along the edge of the corn-fields, hunting for ground-cherries. (MA 31)

The real nature of the ground-cherry is expressed in *O Pioneers!* (p. 29). The berries are closely related to the tomato, and one must use care to eat them only when they are yellow and fully ripe; otherwise they show the unpleasant nature of the nightshade family and can cause some stomach distress.

When fully ripe, with a bit of acid added to combat their blandness, they make splendid preserves, and that, the preserve, is the heart of the story of vegetables, fruits, and berries on the plains frontier. Cather tells us in the passage below not only about the ground-cherry but also about the importance of canning and preserving:

Alexandra often said that if her mother were cast upon a desert island, she would thank God for her deliverance, make a garden, and find something to preserve. Preserving was almost a mania with Mrs. Bergson. Stout as she was, she roamed the scrubby banks of Norway Creek looking for fox grapes and goose plums, like a wild creature in search of prey. She made a yellow jam of the insipid ground-cherries that grew on the prairie, flavoring it with lemon peel; and she made a sticky dark conserve of garden tomatoes. She had experimented even with the rank buffalo-pea, and she could not see a fine bronze cluster of them without shaking her head and murmuring, "What a pity!" When there was nothing more to preserve, she began to pickle. The amount of sugar she used in these processes was sometimes a serious drain upon the family resources. She was a good mother, but she was glad when her children were old enough not to be in her way in the kitchen. She had never quite forgiven John Bergson for bringing her to the end of the earth; but, now that she was there, she wanted to be let alone to reconstruct her old life in so far as that was possible. She could still take some comfort in the world if she had bacon in the cave, glass jars on the shelves, and sheets in the press. (OP 29–30)

The following recipe for ground-cherry preserves was shared with us by Alice Styskal:

Wash cherries. Make a syrup of one pound of sugar and one and one half cups of water. How much syrup you make depends on how many cherries you have. Cut the cherries as fine as you can or grind them. Pack them into hot jars in layers with a little sugar between each layer. Then pour your hot syrup over the cherries, cover and finish in boiler.

The only passage I find that deals with the drying of food-stuffs—certainly the most practical method for the plains—is in *My Ántonia,* and not surprisingly it deals with the unconventional pair Peter and Pavel:

That day the floor was covered with garden things, drying for winter; corn and beans and fat yellow cucumbers. There were no screens or window-blinds in the house, and all the doors and windows stood wide open, letting in flies and sunshine alike. (MA 36)

Bugs were a part of pioneer life that is mentioned in oral histories, folklore, and journals with distressing frequency. I was once asked by another winemaker what could be done about the spiders, bugs, worms, and dirt that are an inevitable part of any cluster of grapes, wild or domestic. The answer is simple: crush the grapes at night.

To some extent, fresh vegetables could be kept fresh in a fruit cellar without preserving. They were sometimes packed in dry straw to aid preservation, or wrapped in newspapers. Even after vegetables, fruits, and root crops were safely harvested from the earth, from bushes, or from trees, they might face new dangers in the cellar:

Claude told Mahailey he was going to the cellar to put up the swinging shelf she had been wanting, so that the rats couldn't get at her vegetables. (OO 19)

Fruits and vegetables were preserved by natural capacity for storage (winter melons, squash, pumpkins), by canning (plums, apricots, and cherries) by fermentation or alcohol (wines and some compotes), and by brining (all manner of pickles). Pickles, those items preserved by being immersed in a salt brine or vinegar, are generally thought of as being cucumber pickles, and there are plenty of examples of cucumber pickles in Cather's plains works (for example, OO 144 or OO 12). The former example even carries with it a hint of the techniques used for preparation when Mrs. Wheeler shouts to Mahailey, as she is pickling cucumbers, "You won't let my vinegar burn, will you?"

For many the word *pickles* is synonymous with *cucumber pickles* and even more specifically *dilled cucumber pickles*. Small wonder, then, that we found such a treasure of dilled cucumber pickles at almost every level of our research. The following two recipes for cucumber pickles and small cucumbers are from the Cathers' copy of Mrs. Lea's *Domestic Cookery* (p. 157).

Gather the cucumbers while they are small, lay them in a jar with salt enough to make a pickle; pour in a little water, and if there is not salt enough to cover them, in a few days put in more. At the end of two weeks put them in a kettle, with cabbage leaves around and through them; fill it up with weak vinegar, and let them scald three hours; put all in a jar for three days, then take out the cucumbers, pour out the vinegar and leaves; put them back in the jar, with some cloves, peppers, horse-radish and mustard; boil some strong vinegar and pour over them.

Wash small cucumbers from two to four inches long; put a gallon of very strong vinegar in a large jar, with mustard seed, scraped horse-radish, and celery seed, a small portion of each, and a tea-cupful of salt; put the cucumbers in the jar; tie them close. Martina's [*sic*] may be pickled the same way, or in the old way of pickling cucumbers.

Cheri Underwood shared the following recipe for crock dills with us:

3 qts water
⅓ c vinegar
½ c canning salt
1 tsp alum

Wash pickles & cut off stems. Place in crock with one handful fresh or dried dill and large clove garlic. Grape leaves may be added on top after above solution is poured in. Cover with plate & put a weight on top like heavy jar. Cover with tea towel. Every few days remove scum. (I don't. I wait a week.) Ready to eat in one week to 10 days. Chili peppers can be added for zing.

To can in jars, just put dill pickles in jar—make fresh brine, seal in jars.

The next three recipes—for dill pickles, dill summer pickles, and plain pickles—were contributed by Alice Styskal:

Pick two pails of cucumbers or enough to fill a five-gallon keg. Put the cucumbers in cold water. This should be done in the evening. While the cucumbers are soaking, make a brine of salt and water strong enough to float an egg. Wash the cucumbers well and put them into the brine. In the morning, take the cucumbers out of the brine and wipe dry. In a five gallon keg, layer the cucumbers. Between each layer of cucumbers place a layer of dill. Put the cover on tight. Make a brine of one part vinegar to three parts of water. To this add some whole pepper and allspice. Boil at least three minutes, cool and pour on the cucumbers through the bunghole in the top of the keg. Cork tight. These will last a long time if not exposed to the air.

Pick medium-sized cucumbers. Wash well. Line the bottom of a stone jar with green dill and grapevine leaves, put in a layer of cucumbers, then a layer of dill and leaves and so on until you fill the jar. Boil a brine of water and salt and a small amount of sugar, usually a tablespoon to four gallons. Cool and pour over the cucumbers. Put two or three crusts of rye bread on the cucumbers. Cover with a plate and put a stone on top to keep the pickles in the water and put away in a cool place. They are ready to eat in a week and taste best when about two weeks old.

Pick and wash cucumbers in the morning. Put them in a stone jar. Make a brine of water and enough salt to float an egg. Pour hot over the cucumbers, add dill seed or the plant itself. Cover with a plate and stone and put in a cool place. In three or four days, put cucumbers in glass jars, cover with boiled vinegar and seal jars.

The following recipe for sweet pickles is a real curiosity from the Cather papers. It is an undated letter to *Home Circle* magazine and is signed "A Bohemian girl, Webster Co."

Pick out small cucumbers and pour over them some hot water, and let stand for four hours. Then boil one gallon of vinegar, one cup of sugar, one cup of salt, a teaspoonful of cream of tartar (which is good to keep the pickles green), one ounce of whole cinnamon, and one tablespoon of cloves together for fifteen minutes; then take the pickles out of the water and put in jars and pour over them the hot vinegar and tighten the jars and put away. I wish some more of the young girls would write.

Cather also mentions green tomato pickles (a delight to the palate that is an abomination to the imagination and which is dealt with elsewhere in these pages), watermelon pickles (my favorites and also dealt with above), and, curiously, pickled onions and pickled peaches, dishes I have not found mentioned elsewhere in pioneer materials.

The following recipe for onion pickles was contributed by Mrs. Viola Schumm of Red Cloud:

Boil some water with salt, pour it over the onions hot, let stand all night. Then peel and put them into cold salt and water. Boil double-distilled vinegar with white spice and when cold put your onions in a jar and pour vinegar over them; tie them tight down with leather. Mind always to keep pickles tied down close or they will spoil.

Mrs. Styskal helped us with a recipe for pickled peaches:

For this you will need eight pounds of ripe but hard clingstone peaches. Rub off the down with a dry cloth. Make a syrup of four pounds of sugar, two ounces of whole cinnamon and a quart of vinegar. Boil this syrup for five minutes. Take each peach and stick two whole cloves into each one. Put into the boiling syrup and boil until tender. Take out the peaches, put them into jars. Boil down the syrup a little and pour over the peaches, and then finish in the boiler.

Garden produce and berries and fruits gathered from hillsides, ditches, and creeks were a source of sweetness on the sugar-starved pioneer plains—and a source too of vitamins that were scarce during long winters. While there are complaints of the burden of cost that the need for added sugar put on pioneer households, the fact of the matter is that there was ample return on the investment: the boiling down of the fruit took major advantage of the natural sugars that were already in the produce. Thus for the investment of a pound of sugar, there might be a return of a pound and a half.

Corncobs are sweet. Their smoke is deliciously sweet for curing hams and bacon. These days they are being ground up and included in cattle feed. In pioneer Nebraska cobs were boiled down to a sweet syrup that was harder to obtain but finer flavored than sorghum molasses. A similar product was corncob jelly, one of the prettiest-colored and delicately flavored jellies imaginable.

Professor Dudley Bailey of the University of Nebraska–Lincoln English Department shared the following recipe with me, with these introductory comments:

Lloyd Petersen was a student of mine, fall, 1975; he brought me this recipe from his grandmother after Thanksgiving that year. Frankly, I found the first batch rather bad, so I added some lemon juice to this second batch—it's not precisely in keeping with pioneer tradition, but it's more nearly edible, I think.

I also found that it took less boiling than grandma suggests; she may like what my mother called "leathery" jelly.

12 corn cobs

6 cups of water

1 package of pectin [The pioneer housewife might have used slightly green apples for pectin]

3 cups of sugar

Break up the cobs into thirds or fourths. Add the water and cook on top of the stove for twenty minutes with the lid left on the pot. Measure three cups of the juice from this and add one package of powdered pectin. Dissolve. Let this come to a boil and then add three cups of sugar. Boil fifteen minutes or until it begins to jell. Pour into jars and let cool. Then seal.

Among Cather's ample inventory of jellies, jams, and preserves are wild grape (OO 66), cherries (MA 193, 338), plums (NR 97, MA 338), strawberries (MA 338, OO 82), crabapples (MA 338), and apricots (OP 194).

Mrs. Berniece Pelt has contributed the following four recipes, beginning with a recipe for elderberry and grape jelly. This is a more likely combination than one might initially expect. Elderberries are so low in acid that anything made of them may taste insipid or medicinal. Wild grapes and some domestics, on the other hand, are often so highly acidic that they must be worked with gloved hands. In recipes they therefore balance each other almost perfectly:

Use one-third of ripe grapes and two-thirds ripe elderberries. Remove the stems, place the fruit in a kettle and cook slowly until tender enough to yield all the juice easily; then pour into the jelly bag and let drain. For each pint of juice add one pint of granulated sugar. Boil the sugar and juice together and stir until the sugar is dissolved. Continue boiling until a little of the jelly, cooled on a saucer, stiffens to the desired consistency.

Rhubarb was a popular pioneer plant because it was so versatile, providing a base for sauce, pie, wine, or jelly; because it is up early in the spring, when the palate lusts for the taste of the season; and because it grows well on the plains.

From Mrs. Mary Lambrecht of Red Cloud:

Six pounds of rhubarb
Add six pounds of sugar
Add six large lemons

Cut rhubarb into small pieces about one inch. Lemons should be sliced, and the peel cut very fine, removing the seeds. Put the fruit into a large bowl, cover with sugar. Let stand twenty-four hours. Put all in a large pan and boil it slowly for about three-quarters of an hour. Taking care it does not stick to pan. Also not stir so much as to break the pieces of rhubarb, as the beauty of it is in being whole. (Note it is equal parts of rhubarb and sugar so you can use cups, pounds, or bouls [*sic*]. Cut down lemons to 3 if cups are used.)

Jam should spin a thread when ready to put in hot sterilized jars, and sealed. (Can be sealed with paraffin wax.)

RASPBERRY-RHUBARB
2 cups fresh raspberries
4 cups rhubarb
6 cups sugar
Put ingredients on the stove and cook until it is of the consistency of marmalade or fruit butter.

CHERRY PRESERVES:
2 pounds pitted cherries
2 pounds sugar
Combine cherries and sugar. Heat slowly to boiling. Boil 8 minutes. Let stand over night. Pack without heating into sterilized jars.

Between the pages of the Cathers' *White House Cook Book* we found the following recipe for plum jam, torn from page 9 of the September, 1909, issue of *Woman's World*:

Wash, dry and weigh the plums; allow three-quarters of their weight in sugar; put the plums over the fire and boil gently for three-quarters of an hour, stirring often to prevent burning. Remove the stones as they rise to the surface and crack one-quarter of them. At the end of three-quarters of an hour put in the sugar and continue to boil the jam for fifteen minutes, stirring constantly and removing all scum as it rises. Five minutes before it is done put in the kernels. When partly cool place in jars.

The next recipe, for plum jelly, was from an undated and untitled newspaper clipping found between the pages of the Cathers' *Home Queen Cook Book*:

This jelly is very nice and can be made from large or small plums; it jells easier than most other fruit. Cook and drain through a jelly bag; measure, and allow one pound of granulated sugar for each pint of juice; heat the sugar and add, cooking from twelve to fifteen minutes, then test.

The next two recipes, for crabapple jelly and peach preserves, are from a column titled "The Heart of the House" by Marion R. Howland in *Woman's World,* September, 1909:

Wash the apples, cut in small pieces and place in kettle with just enough water to cover them. Place on the stove and cook to a pulp. Put into a jelly bag and allow to drain but do not squeeze, as it will allow some of the pulp to go through and spoil the jelly. To each pint of juice allow a pound of sugar and boil together for twenty minutes, or until a little of the juice, cooled, forms a jelly. If for any reason the jelly should not be as firm as desired, by placing in the direct sunlight for a short time it will be improved greatly.

Have ready a kettle of boiling water. Place the peaches in a wire basket and plunge into the boiling water. In two minutes take them out and the skins will rub off easily. Drop the fruit in cold water to keep the color. For three pounds of fruit use one pound of sugar and one pint of water for three pounds of sugar. When the syrup is boiling hot take the fruit from the water and drop into it. Put a few at a time, as they cook rapidly. Take from the syrup with a silver fork and place in the jar, filling the vessel to the brim with the syrup. Do not remove the stones from the peaches, as they give a very fine flavor to the preserves.

Alice Styskal provides general directions for preserves and a specific recipe for strawberries:

Sort your jars carefully, making sure that none are cracked. Make sure you have a lid and a rubber band for each jar. Always use new rubber bands or jar rings, as they don't cost too much and it is cheaper to buy new than to waste the preserve if the jar doesn't seal right. Jars should be scalded and kept hot when you are filling them. Take your boiler for clothes. Place wood laths on bottom of boiler. Fill hot jars on wood laths, leaving a little space between jars. Pour warm water into the boiler until it reaches an inch below the lower edge of the covers. Bring to a boil and boil for ten minutes. Carefully take out the jars and tighten the lids. When cool, store in a cool dry place.

Pick and sort your strawberries so that you have at least twelve quarts of firm, ripe berries. Wash and drain them well. In an enameled kettle, boil two pounds of white sugar and a half cup of water. Boil this ten minutes. Then add the berries and boil about twenty five minutes, without stirring so that you don't mash the fruit. Skim the foam off the top often. Take out the berries with a skimmer and put into your hot jars. Boil the syrup down until thick and pour over the berries until the jars are full. Put the jars into your boiler and proceed as above.

For Czechs like Ántonia, the preserves were merely a stage toward a later and more important goal: *kolaches*! The jams and preserves, wonderful enough as they were from the jar, could be stretched (an important concept in pioneer cookery) by being incorporated and recooked on a bread base.

Gardens and Orchards

When Cather speaks of the basic elements of survival on the Great Plains—shelter, food, water—she adds another that we often neglect these hundred years later: the garden. Today it is "nice" to have a garden, a kind of frivolous activity one does for amusement. For Cather's cooks the garden was the foundation of the family's meals. The Shimerda's predicament here at the End of the Earth was couched in terms of a garden:

they had come to live on a wild place where there was no garden. . . . (MA 19)

It is understood that should they survive the winter, a cow, chickens, and a garden in the spring would provide the basis for enduring the next assault of a plains winter.

The last words of John Bergson include the provision that his widow be permitted to plant her garden and set her orchard; he obviously understood wherein the power of his legacy lay:

"Don't grudge your mother a little time for plowing her garden and setting out fruit trees, even if it comes in a busy season. She has been a good mother to you, and she has always missed the old country." (OP 27–28)

Even in town Mrs. Harling has her garden and orchard (MA 147, 193)

What grows in the gardens of Cather's characters? The variety is great: cabbage (OP 187), pumpkins and potatoes (MA 16), melons (OP 31), sweet potatoes, cucumbers, citrons, asparagus, gooseberries, currants (OP 48–49), and even domesticated sunflowers (OP 88). In Mrs. Bergson's garden there are also zinnias, marigolds, and scarlet sage. The sage can be interpreted as a spice or pomander filling, but what do we make of zinnias and marigolds? Beauty amidst function? A luxury among necessity? Today gardeners often still plant these flowers within or around a food garden as an insect repellant, and it could be that Cather has subtlely reminded us of this traditional technique of garden culture.

We don't often think of the plains farm in terms of orchards, but there was a time when Nebraska was the Tree Planter State and farmers throughout the Great Plains enriched their lives and larders with carefully tended orchards. Ragged remnants of those orchards can still be found at old plains farms, but few today are maintained and even fewer are being planted. The assumption seems to be that there is little sense in planting for the future, for there may be no future. Our children probably won't want this farm anyway, the reasoning seems to be, and even if they do, they won't want to take care of an orchard. But there was a time when everything was for the children and it was understood that the children would grow up with the same sorts of needs—and common sense—as their parents.

What grew in Cather's orchards? Apples and cherries are most common (MA 193, MA 341, OP 104, OP 151, OP 152, OO 25, OP 81, MA 339–40, OP 133), but there are grape arbors (MA 340), mulberries (OP 134, OP 83, MA 341, OP 152, OP 153, MA 339—here planted in a hedge to protect the more delicate cherry and apple trees), crabapples (MA 341, MA 353), apricots (OP 151, OP 136—a beautiful passage that demonstrates the emotional fruit that trees can bear), walnuts (OP 84), gooseberries and currants (MA 339), and finally the orchard, with its abundant, sweet-nectared flowers, the obvious shelter for the hives of the bees (OO 205, OP 84).

The authors of this book have a tree farm and are perhaps excessively attracted and attached to trees, but Cather's passages about orchards that strike most closely to our hearts are those that speak of the human relationships to trees, the feelings that people have—or had—for trees. Carl Linstrum says of his father's orchard:

"I wish I had a dollar for every bucket of water I've carried for those trees. Poor father, he was an easy man, but he was perfectly merciless when it came to watering the orchard." (OP 133)

And Alexandra responds,

"That's one thing I like about Germans; they make an orchard grow if they can't make anything else. I'm so glad these trees belong to some one [*sic*] who takes comfort in them." (OP 133)

Marie Shabata pursues the logic of that affection for trees to its most vivid and powerful expression:

"I'm a good Catholic, but I think I could get along with caring for trees, if I had n't anything else."

"That's a poor saying," said Emil. . . .

"Why is it? If I feel that way, I feel that way. I like trees because they seem more resigned to the way they have to live than other things do. I feel as if this tree knows everything I ever think of when I sit here. When I come back to it, I never have to remind it of anything; I begin just where I left off." (OP 153)

In the days of frontier self-sufficiency, each family, rural and urban, would convert its lawn into a grocery store, its landscaping into a farm:

Grandmother often said that if she had to live in town, she thanked God she lived next the Harlings. They had been farming people, like ourselves, and their place was like a little farm, with a big barn and a garden, and an orchard and grazing lots—even a windmill. (MA 147)

Again and again Cather refers to the activities of the orchard, its constant demand on the energies of the owners (OP 83, MA 193). I have always taken pleasure in the fact that my favorite of Cather's people, Ántonia, has the finest and most comforting of orchards. Comforting because the real bounty of an orchard is not alone in its harvest but in its promise of harvest, the shade and cool and sense of order that it brought to the plains:

At some distance behind the house were an ash grove and two orchards: a cherry orchard, with gooseberry and currant bushes between the
rows, and an apple orchard, sheltered by a high hedge from the hot winds.
The older children turned back when we reached the hedge, but Jan and
Nina and Lucie crept through it by a hole known only to themselves and
hid under the low-branching mulberry bushes.

As we walked through the apple orchard, grown up in tall bluegrass,
Ántonia kept stopping to tell me about one tree and another. "I love them as
if they were people," she said, rubbing her hand over the bark. "There
wasn't a tree here when we first came. We planted every one, and used to
carry water for them, too—after we'd been working in the fields all
day." . . . There was the deepest peace in that orchard. It was surrounded
by a triple enclosure; the wire fence, then the hedge of thorny locusts, then
the mulberry hedge which kept out the hot winds of summer and held fast
to the protecting snows of winter. The hedges were so tall that we could see
nothing but the blue sky above them, neither the barn roof nor the windmill. The afternoon sun poured down on us through the drying grape
leaves. The orchard seemed full of sun, like a cup, and we could smell the
ripe apples on the trees. The crabs hung on the branches as thick as beads on
a string, purple-red, with a thin silvery glaze over them. (MA 339–41)

Two berries dominate Cather's writing, the mulberry and the
cherry. Mulberries came to the plains as part of early efforts to
develop a silk industry. They were eaten mostly out of hand, the
rich, juicy berries providing a fine afternoon treat. In this regard, I
had never quite understood one of Cather's passages:

He reached up among the [white mulberry] branches and began to pick the
sweet, insipid fruit. . . . (OP 153)

I have eaten mulberries throughout my life, and I would not characterize them as being so sweet as to be insipid. Until I found a white
mulberry tree on our farm and at a couple of handfuls of its berries
one June. The fruit was indeed so candy-sweet that only a little bit of
it could be eaten before it was just too much.

If mulberries represent the wild bounty of berries, then
cherries are the domestic gift. Again and again Cather writes of
picking and preserving cherries (OP 104, 151, MA 193). One of the
bitterest passages in *One of Ours* has Claude Wheeler's father re-

John Polnicky's Saloon, Red Cloud, Nebraska

sponding to his wife's complaint that the cherries of the orchard are beyond her reach by cutting down the precious tree. The reader instantly hates the man from the moment of that passage (oo 25–26).

Drink

Within some pioneer families the only drink other than whole milk or buttermilk was "Adam's ale" (water) but during the hot summer, especially at haying or threshing season, there was need or use for other thirst quenchers. A favorite then that is still a favorite of ours now is sun tea. It is simply iced tea, but there is something about the process that definitely produces a different, much better flavor. It is not a difficult process. Fill a glass jar—quart, half-gallon, or gallon—with water. Add loose tea (herb tea or tea leaves, but not instant tea) in the customary amount for your taste, or slightly more. Some prefer at this stage to add a small amount of sugar. Put a loose lid on the jar and let it sit outside in the sun for several hours. Strain and ice this infusion and see if it isn't the best iced tea you've ever drunk.

"Switchel" or "haying switchel" was a traditional drink in the fields. It was usually carried in a stone or glass jug covered with heavy layers of wet burlap to keep it cool. If it was made a day ahead of use it would acquire a little fizz (and a slight alcoholic kick) from the short fermentation. It was not unusual for a haying crew to add a little bit of corn liquor or whiskey during the noon break so that the afternoon rests and the ride home were a little happier than might have been expected from bone-weary men. This recipe is from our own recipe files:

> ¾ to 1 cup of brown sugar
> ¼ to ½ cup of molasses
> ½ teaspoon ginger
> ¾ cup vinegar
> 2 quarts of water
> Mix this thoroughly, especially the ginger, and ice well.

Many pioneer households made wine, often for medicinal application. The pioneer wine maker was forced to use the materials he found around him, even though they were not the kind of things he had worked with in the Old Country.

Yet sometimes the final results required no apologies at all. Wild fox grapes still grow along plains river banks, and in a good year the heavy clusters of blue to almost black grapes will cause tree branches to break off. These small berries are very high in flavor and color and therefore are well suited to dilution or blending with other wild berries, especially elderberries, to a dilution of 50 percent. This is a recipe I developed during my own wine-making career:

> 8 pounds of wild grapes, stemmed and crushed
> 1 gallon of water
> 3 or 3½ pounds of sugar thoroughly dissolved in the water and grape juice
> yeast (a small amount of commercial bread yeast will do and this is what was often used by pioneer winemakers but I prefer a good

wine yeast purchased at a wine-hobbiest shop. It is definitely not the pioneer way but it is so much work picking grapes that I hate to see the effort go to waste. You might also want to wear protective gloves when working with the grapes; they are very acidic and can irritate the skin.)

Put this in a cool but not cold place, cover with a tight cloth and stir thoroughly twice a day. At the end of five days strain out the grapes and let the wine continue until fermentation ceases. Siphon the wine into a bottle or barrel stoppered with a tight wad of cotton batting until all signs of fermentation have stopped and the wine has settled. Then cork or lid tightly. This wine, with a little age on it, is as mellow as black velvet.

I never think of wild-grape wine without remembering a passage from Mari Sandoz's *Old Jules* (p. 350):

> For supper they had *Weinschnitte*. Mary dipped the slices of bread lightly in wild grape wine and into egg batter and fried them brown in butter. While still hot she sprinkled them with cinnamon and sugar and piled them high on a big platter.

For white wine the basic plant was often rhubarb. It has plenty of the acids so necessary to a good wine and makes a wine that can be surprisingly close to German and French white wines—which must have been a comfort to German and French migrants to the plains:

> 3–5 pounds of rhubarb (depending on how strong you want the wine to taste)
>
> 1 gallon of water
>
> 3 pounds of sugar

Cut the rhubarb into inch-long segments and put in a crock. Cover with sugar and let stand for a day. Add water and a half-spoon of yeast. Let this ferment in a covered crock in a cool place for five days, stirring thoroughly twice a day and then remove the rhubarb pulp. Siphon the juice into a jug and stopper with a wad of cotton batting. When the fermentation has totally ceased and the wine has settled, siphon it into bottles and stopper— if it has absolutely stopped its bubbling. Age a few months and drink.

I had every expectation that I would open the discussion of drink in Cather's works with an essay on coffee, but the fact of the matter is that while coffee does indeed form an important part of

Cather's inventory of potables, it is alcoholic drinks that dominate. And as might be expected there is that strange ambiguity that alcohol represents in our culture: it is simultaneously the most civilizing and the most debasing of influences.

There was already a growing movement for temperance (actually, abstinence) in the nineteenth-century Nebraska towns Cather describes in works like *My Ántonia* and *O Pioneers!* and yet there remained traces of the European understanding that alcohol was not an opponent of religion but its ally. That curious relationship that men and women and alcohol have on the rural plains was already developing: men drink in the bars, women resent it. Women do not join their men; they are not always welcome. The more firmly the women state their ultimatums, the more firmly the men cling to their bar stools. The wife's telephone call to the town bar has become a part of plains folklore, as has the husband's ignoring of it. A common sign in such taverns reads:

> Phone answering charges:
> "He ain't here" = $1
> "Ain't seem him all day" = $2
> "Where's that rascal been this past month?" = $4
> "Who?" = $10

Cather describes a puny salesman, rebuffed from his advances to a peasant farm woman larger and stronger than he, retreating to the saloon to drink some courage (OP 7–9). Johnnie Gardener drinks with his guests until he becomes "rather absent-minded" (MA 182) and later sums up his situation with words that could be said for half my friends in Dannebrog: "'S a fact, boys. . . . If I take a drink in Black Hawk, Molly knows it in Omaha!" (MA 190–91)

The conflict between alcohol as the Water of Life, the Blood of Christ, the stuff over which toasts are made, and the destroyer of the family, the Demon Rum, can be seen in a vignette from *One of Ours* (pp. 165–66), the marriage of Claude and Enid. Just as the bride and groom constitute a contrast in styles, so too does the wedding. The vegetarian bride is toasted (I can scarcely write it I am so appalled) in grape juice, but the father of the bride, once the guests are seated, takes the father of the groom to the fruit cellar, "where the two old friends drank off a glass of well-seasoned Kentucky whiskey, and shook hands."

Cather is not noted for a rapier wit, but to my own taste it is all the more splendid, like my wife Linda's, because it is distributed with reserve and is so subtle that the victim has bled to death before noticing the wound. It is like the wedding passage in *One of Ours*. When the two gentlemen return to the party, "looking younger than when they withdrew," the attending minister smells the alcohol and feels slighted:

He looked disconsolately into his ruddy goblet and thought about the marriage at Cana. He tried to apply his Bible literally to life and, though he didn't dare breathe it aloud in these days, he could never see why he was better than his Lord. (OO 166)

For those of us who can understand someone's having an aversion to alcohol but who are baffled by any New Testament rationale, those few lines are worth learning by rote.

Just as individuals made (and make) their choice about alcoholic drinks, so too did (and do) plains towns. Since about 90 percent of the business, social life, and information exchange take place at the Eric's Big Table Tavern in Dannebrog, it has always been hard to imagine how such things are done in "dry" towns; that's the way it was on Cather's frontier too (MA 179).

Cather's attitudes toward Prohibition are only thinly disguised. She gives her most distasteful characters a bent toward the movement and her most solid heroes and heroines an aversion or indifference toward it. Bayliss' attitude in *One of Ours* is a sardonic representation of what Cather saw to be a good part of the motivation of the Prohibitionists:

Bayliss had a social as well as a hygienic prejudice against alcohol, and he hated it less for the harm it did than for the pleasure it gave. (OO 182)

Enid's zeal lent her a rudeness that turned away her husband's old friends:

Ernest Havel came to see Claude now, but not often. They both felt it would be indelicate to renew their former intimacy. Ernest still felt aggrieved about his beer, as if Enid had snatched the tankard from his lips with her own corrective hand. (OO 195)

That zeal in moral causes is seen as a symbol of her coldness and perversity in all things of life, including sex. She even denies her hens their roosters (OO 174–75).

Beer was the standard drink and was served in saloons and gardens throughout the Great Plains. While beer is thought of, with reason, as being a German or Czech product, Cather describes a wedding in the French community as being well supplied with barrels of beer. (OP 82) She leaves us with the impression that it was nonetheless the Germans and especially the Czechs who saw beer, as did our Pilgrim forefathers, as "liquid bread," a standard part of the worker's diet. It was the German and Czech farmers who brought their lunches into the Czech saloon in Black Hawk, "admitted, even by the church people, to be as respectable as a saloon could be" (MA 217).

Hundreds of small-town bars throughout the Great Plains are still like this and merit the traveler's attention. Why eat fast food, always the same, when you can stop in a Czech, German, or Norwegian tavern and experience genuine regional culture? It was the Czech Frank Shabata who "set all the Bohemian girls in a flutter" and who was "easily the buck of the beer-gardens" (OP 143). A visitor asks for beer at a Norwegian threshing bee and is told to go to the Bohemians for beer because "the Norwegians didn't have none when they threshed." (OP 177–78)

There is a sense of logical as well as grammatical progression in the statement that "Ernest Havel was a Bohemian, and he usually drank a glass of beer when he came to town" (OO 10–11). Her husband, Cuzak, tells us one of the reasons the warm and mellow Ántonia is such an attractive wife:

Sometimes maybe I drink a little too much beer in town, and when I come home she don't say nothing. She don't ask me no questions. (MA 365–66)

Beer was not served only in the saloons. A household might keep beer in the cellar just as surely as flour or potatoes. In *My Ántonia,* Mr. Harling keeps beer in his cellar (p. 206), Mr. Tovesky enjoys a bottle of beer and a pipe of tobacco before he retires in *O Pioneers!* (p. 144), and one of the things Mrs. Lee misses during her stay at Lou's house is her beer (OP 95). As a man of strong tastes myself, I think often and warmly of a comforting passage in *My Ántonia*:

Before [Mr. Harling] went to bed [Mrs. Harling] always got him a lunch of smoked salmon or anchovies and beer. (MA 157)

The beer of Cather's frontier was not like modern beer. It was heavier, less effervescent, with much more flavor and nutrition than the pallid and anemic wash marketed today. It came in corked bottles or bottles with replacable ceramic caps. It had a dark amber color and about the same alcoholic content as modern beers, give or take a percentage point or two (about 4 percent). Modern drinkers are sometimes appalled to hear that the English and Germans drink their beer at room temperature. They curl their lips at the aspect of warm beer. There are two mitigating factors, however: first, the allusion is to *cellar* temperature rather than *room* temperature, and in England and Germany that is closer to fifty-five degrees than seventy-five. Such beers are brewed to be drunk warmer. Modern American beers taste terrible when they are warm because they are brewed to be drunk cold. European beers are brewed to be drunk warmer and are extraordinarily good at fifty-five or sixty-five degrees.

Many of the beers of Cather's imagination, experience, and writing were assuredly homemade. A couple of pounds of malted barley was cracked, run through a mill or smashed under a rolling pin, and cooked into a gallon of water. A tea of hops (imported dry or grown on the farm itself; I have seen several old Nebraska farms where hops patches still thrive) was added to contribute a balancing tartness, along with a quarter-pound of sugar or molasses per gallon. Bread yeast was sometimes used to inoculate the wort, as unfermented beer is called, but some home brewers kept a culture of true beer yeast growing in a jar in the cupboard or dried on a paddle or small broom. The beer was allowed to ferment in a cool basement or cellar in a crock or barrel for a couple of days, until the vigorous action had ceased, and then it was bottled. It was usually capped when there was just enough "action" left to give it a slight fizz. Beer was not as carbonated then as now because of taste. Besides, it was a matter of safety: too much fizz can cause bottles to explode like munitions.

It is often too troublesome or difficult to make or obtain genuine brewing malts today, so it has become the habit of modern home brewers to use canned syrups, obtainable in most large supermarkets. I have been told that these syrups gained popularity during Prohibition, when the cans carried a warning label that the purchaser should be careful not to mix the can of syrup with five gallons of water, three pounds of sugar, and yeast, keeping the mixture in a covered crock for three to five days, because the result would be beer, which was of course illegal.

It is impossible to make a fine beer out of canned malt syrup, but it is easy and traditional and one can acquire a taste for the result. The first home brew I ever tasted, in the Wyoming farm home of my Uncle Fred and Aunt Mary, was made from Blue Ribbon Malt Syrup and even today I can remember the taste, sweetened by its being forbidden.

One of the most interesting social experiments I have ever conducted happened almost by accident during my own decade of home brewing. I found that any time I went into a store and bought a can of malt syrup, a sack of sugar, and a package of yeast, the grocery clerk or the person behind me in line would have something to say, such as "Add a potato; it'll clear up the beer" or "Put a light bulb under the crock to keep it warm at night." It became a game: I would go to the checkout counter where a little old lady was holding sway and where the bagger was a ten-year-old boy. They would both have something to say: "Add a cup of rice and it'll be stronger" or "Add a half-pound of brown sugar." The tradition of home brewing is alive and well in the American household.

Cather reports Wick Cutter's boast that he never drank anything stronger than sherry (MA 209) and has champagne being
served as a stage prop at a Lincoln production (MA 273). But those
are Cather's symbols of Cutter's smallness and Lincoln's sophistication. The wines of Cather's plains novels are homemade. There are
not the kinds of grapes here for wines that the settlers had known in
Europe. Vinifera grapes (wine grapes) grow in Europe, but not in
America; here we find *labrusca,* or fox grapes, which produce a
strange off-taste, like our grape juice, and which are best suited for
jellies.

Wild grapes, however, which still grow in abundance along
plains creeks and rivers (although not in the quantity common to
Cather's time) can be coaxed into a wonderful heavy wine like East
European "Bull's Blood." Rosicky took along a bottle of his wild-
grape wine on the occasion of a picnic celebrating his family's wealth
in spite of that year's crop failure (NR 98). In *O Pioneers!* (p. 52),
Alexandra speaks of a communal family effort of making wild-
plum wine (p. 52), and Anna Hansen in *My Ántonia* (p. 232) makes
elderblow (elderflower) wine.

Wild grapes and plums are very high in taste and acid and
therefore make good wine. In fact, they are so high in natural acids
that they may irritate your hands as you work with them. It may
seem to you that there is precious little pulp compared to pit in the
fruit, but since you can add quite a bit of water to that pulp, it makes
more wine than might be expected. This recipe is from our own files
and has been notably successful:

Crush the fruit (but not the pits or seeds) and to each eight to twelve
pounds add one gallon of water and mix thoroughly. Add about two
pounds of completely dissolved sugar to each gallon of mixture and mix
thoroughly. If you can obtain it, add a good wine yeast according to in-
structions on the package. Let the mixture ferment in a crock or clean barrel
for a week or so until the violent fermentation ceases. Stir twice daily. Pour
off the wine, feed the pulp to your hogs or chickens and let the wine sit in a
barrel or large jugs until all fermentation stops and the wine settles clear. At
this point add another half pound of sugar per gallon if you want a sweeter

wine and let the wine re-ferment and settle. Bottle and store for a few months or years.

Yeast is funny stuff. It is not really an ingredient, so it is not possible to give proportions. It is a living organism, and when it is put into a favorable environment—bread dough, beer wort, or wine must—it multiplies to the point where it saturates the mixture. And there are different kinds of yeast. Bread yeast is not beer yeast; bread yeast is bred and refined to make nice little bubbles in dough, and beer yeast is designed to convert malt sugars into alcohol. Beer yeast produces a flavor that is not favorable for wine. And wild yeasts (the light haze that blushes the surface of grapes and plums and is in the air all around us all the time) is very unpredictable. It can produce all sorts of off-flavors wherever it is dominant. It is always best to use a yeast especially cultured for a particular purpose.

Elderblow wine is a very delicate wine and a bit more difficult to make. Gather elderflowers (they grow in monstrous, creamy, perfumed heads) and to each gallon of flowers add a gallon of warm water with two and a half pounds of sugar dissolved in each gallon. When the mixture cools, add a good wine yeast (according to its directions) and let the mixture ferment for three days, stirring it twice a day. At the end of three days, remove the blooms. Let the wine ferment until it is still and then siphon off into clean jugs or a barrel. Allow the wine to finish fermenting and to settle clear, and then let it age a few months before drinking.

Such wines were potable, but not what the European settlers in particular were used to. Indeed, there are people yet today who feel that nothing should properly be called wine unless it is made with vinifera grapes. Frontier wines were often a little too strong in taste or a little too weak, a trifle off, a bit thin, musty, musky, or what-ever. But it was too good to throw away, and it was all there was. In such cases the wine was mulled, or spiced.

Mulled wines were usually served hot and made a fine, hearty winter refreshment, still carrying many of the flavors and nutrients of summer. Mulled wine has to be made to taste, so you will have to work out your own formula. Mulled wines are usually sweet, so add roughly a cup of sugar to each quart or two of hot wine. While heating the wine, add a cinnamon stick, cloves, even mints, pepper, or dried fruit.

The following recipe is from page 500 of the Cathers' *Home Queen Cook Book*:

Let the grapes remain on the vines until danger of frost, then gather, place in a barrel which has one head out, set the barrel on end, bore a hole near the bottom and put in it a wooden faucet, cover the bottom of the barrel with clean shucks or straw, fill with the grapes just as gathered, without stemming or bruising them; then fill the barrel with rain water and let stand in a cool place (covered to keep out dust) from 14 to 21 days; then drain off through the faucet and add 1 lb. sugar to each gallon of liquid. When the sugar is dissolved, pour into a tight barrel, cork and seal so that no air can enter the barrel. It will be very good in a few months, but of course grows better all the time. This is as good wine as the best imported. Care should be taken never to bruise the grapes if the native grape is used, as it will spoil the wine.

This recipe for a modest quantity of heavy ginger beer is from page 152 of Mrs. Lea's *Domestic Cookery*:

Put two pounds of brown sugar in a jug, with a heaped spoonful of ginger, and a pint of strong hop tea; pour in a gallon and a half of warm water, and a teacup of yeast; leave out the cork a day—then fasten it up, and set in a cool place; or if you bottle it, put two or three raisins in each bottle.

The following harvest beer is also from Mrs. Lea's, pages 152–53; the porter beer and molasses beer are from page 153:

To make fifteen gallons of beer, put into a keg three pints of yeast, three pints of molasses, and two gallons of cold water; mix it well, and let it stand a few minutes; then take three quarts of molasses, and three gallons of boiling water, with one ounce of ginger; mix them well, and pour into a keg, and fill it up with cold water.

A decoction of the root of sassafras is good to put in beer.

A pleasant drink in summer is to take one bottle of porter, five bottles of water, and a pint of molasses, or a pound of sugar; make a spoonful of ginger into tea, and mix all well together; have seven clean bottles, with two or three raisins in each; fill them, cork them tight, and lay them on their sides on the cellar floor.

Take five pints of molasses, half a pint of yeast, two spoonsful of pounded ginger, and one of allspice; put these into a clean half-barrel, and pour on it two gallons of boiling water; shake it till fermentation is produced; then fill it up with warm water, and let it work with the bung out, a day, when it will be fit for use; remove it to a cold place, or bottle it. This is a very good drink for laboring people in warm weather.

As was the case with wines, there was a wide range between the fine liquors of Europe and the harsh, unforgiving whiskeys of the Great Plains frontier. There were rare occasions when a fine cognac might make an appearance (OP 256) or a Virginia apple brandy (MA 86) or a rare bottle of the nectar-like Benedictine (MA 260). But those were reserved for quiet moments with a good cigar or in a warm den during the cold winter.

More often than not, spirits were taken in quick gulps in a cellar, a cigar serving only to disguise the odor of the drink (read the passage on OO 97 with some imagination). Raw spirits were sometimes doctored to imitate the *Kirsch, Schnapps,* or *Kümmel* of the Old Country:

Three big Bohemians were drinking raw alcohol, tinctured with oil of cinnamon. This was said to fortify one effectually against the cold, and they smacked their lips after each pull at the flask. (OP 13)

Sweet cherry cider, peppermint, or even dried fruit could be added for flavoring to home recipes. My grandmother used to make her own spirits. She would mix *Schnitz* (dried fruit) with water and make a mash, which, set on the back of the stove for a few days, would quickly ferment to a potent soup. She put the mixture in the bottom of her huge Dutch oven on the stove, put a canning rack in it, set a small canning jar in the center, and put the cover back on upside down. The lid's handle knob was thus inside the pot and immediately above the jar. She filled the lid with snow and put the whole apparatus over a slow fire. The alcohol evaporated, hit the cold lid, ran down into the jar, and at the end of a day she had a small amount of potent spirits. She flavored the result with a little grape juice and called it cough medicine.

Of course it worked. When one of the children had a cold and was fussy, a tablespoon (a jigger, that is) or two of the "medicine" would put the little tyke right to sleep. So it is perhaps not at all inappropriate that Rosicky serves the visiting doctor a little drink in a medicine glass (NR 76). Medicine should be administered as medicine.

Spirits were seen as a staple of the temperate housewife's medicine chest. Sometimes they were disguised as patent medicines—some, like Lydia Pinkham's nostrum, were at least as strong as the drunken husband's whiskey—or passed off as nonalcoholic (my father says his mother would probably have been astonished to know how strong her cough medicine was). It was also generally understood that commercial alcohol could serve as the basis for any number of home cures; even today car sickness, a cold, hiccups, hangovers, or a cramped muscle are treated with alcohol toddies, rubs, shots, and snorts.

Alexandra put a weary and sick Emil to bed with some brandy (OP 246), Russian Peter mixed a specific of hot water and whiskey for severe illness (MA 54), and Alexandra calmed and soothed Mrs. Lee with a balm of

a little brandy, with hot water and sugar, before she went to bed, and Alexandra always had it ready for her. "It sends good dreams," she would say with a twinkle in her eye. (OP 189–90)

There were commercial soft drinks (MA 195), iced teas, and switchels. Lemonade was a particular favorite. In case you wonder why, try making real lemonade yourself; you will be surprised at how wonderfully good it is. The recipe is from our own files.

8–10 lemons
sugar to taste
one gallon of cold water
Cut and juice the lemons, add both juice and rinds to water, add and mix in sugar. Serve on ice.

From the Cathers' *Home Queen Cook Book* (p. 499) comes this recipe for English lemonade:

Pare a number of lemons, according to the quantity of drink you wish to make, allowing 1 large lemon to 1 pt. of drink. Pour boiling water on the peels, and let infuse. Boil your sugar to the consistency of cream, in which whip the white of 1 egg. When it boils pour in a little cold water to stop it; then let it boil again, when the pan should be taken off to cool and settle, skimming off any scum that may rise to the top. When settled pour off the syrup into the pee water. [The use of *sic* to indicate that the text is indeed thus is not sufficient, we think, to deal with this textual problem. That last sentence is reproduced precisely as it appears in the cookbook. We hope it should read "peel water."] Now add the juice and as much water as is necessary to make a rich drink. Strain, if wanted to look perfectly clear.

While the pioneer could always make alcohol from wild fruits and berries of the region, distill it in a Dutch oven, or disguise its poor quality with flavorings and spices, it was not so easy to simulate coffee (which, incidentally, could be used medicinally like spirits; see OP 141). Of course there were plenty of efforts to do so. Coffee had to be brought from so far away and was so expensive, after all, that it was frequently stretched with burnt grains (corn, barley, or rye) and roots, especially dandelion or chicory. Just as early travelers on the plains were sure to carry sufficient quantities of whiskey among their stores, they also carried coffee.

Cather describes instances of coffee's being served, at breakfast of course (MA 95), but also in midafternoon (MA 110) and even late into the night (MA 157). She shows it weak (OO 5) and strong (OO 82), with cream (OP 86) and with sugar (OO 5). Perhaps the strongest statement about preference is in *One of Ours*:

"I'll make the coffee good and strong; that will please [Claude] more than anything. (OO 82)

When I think of varying preferences for the strength of coffee, I recall a situation in Minden, Nebraska, when a very nice, gentle pioneer woman was serving coffee—the kind that nice, gentle women seem inclined to, the kind that is generally served in smallish clear-glass cups. As she stepped from the kitchen she asked the group in her front room, "Would anyone like some coffee?" Oscar Henry, a salty old-timer himself, looked at the transparent broth in his "cup" and said, "Yes, do you know where we can get some?"

Among the more sophisticated folks in the city, for those who always seemed to know that enjoyable things are not good for you, coffee of course was also a bane:

When [Bayliss] saw [Mrs. Wheeler] pour a second cup of coffee for herself and for Claude at the end of dinner, he said, in a gentle, grieved tone, "I'm sorry to see you taking two, Mother."

Mrs. Wheeler looked at him over the coffee-pot with a droll, guilty smile. "I don't believe coffee hurts me a particle, Bayliss."

"Of course it does; it's a stimulant." What worse could it be, his tone implied! When you said anything was a "stimulant," you had sufficiently condemned it; there was no more noxious word. (OO 79)

The real message Cather gives us about coffee concerns the Bohemians and their feelings about coffee, an even stronger association than their cultural attachment to spirits and beer. Doctor Burleigh would like to instruct Rosicky to drink less coffee, but he knows better than to suggest that course of treatment:

"You'll do as you choose about that. I've never yet been able to separate a Bohemian from his coffee or his pipe." (NR 73)

When Mrs. Shimerda wants to demonstrate the utterly abject poverty of her family's situation, in the absence of English words to describe it all she grabs her empty coffeepot and shakes it at her visitors, thereby demonstrating the depths to which they had sunk (MA 73); when things are good, coffee is served in big cups (NR 82), strong and rich with cream (NR 75). Just as "coffee and cream" is almost a single word in many vocabularies, Cather suggests to us that for the Bohemians "coffee and *kolaches*" might just as well be one word (NR 82), and in O Pioneers! Marie says it quite explicitly:

"I hope you'll like these, Mrs. Lee. . . . The Bohemians always like them with their coffee." (OP 194)

Coffee was ground in hand grinders and corn mills, was scraped in nutmeg graters, or was pounded to a pulp in the corner of a cloth bag. The real secret to good coffee was perhaps better known a hundred years ago than it is now: never boil it. Should the inventor of percolators, in which coffee is boiled over and over, still be alive and should I ever encounter him, I fully intend to percolate him. It is better just to pour boiling water over ground coffee in a sieve than to percolate it. A pioneer system (still used by campers, who probably wonder why camp coffee tastes better than the poison they brew in their kitchens) was to boil a coffeepot of water and then throw in a handful or two of coffee, immediately taking the pot from the fire. A cup of cold water or a few eggshells thrown into the pot settled the grounds. But the main thing is: coffee is never to be boiled.

Cather mentions tea in two memorable instances in her plains works. In one case a ginger tea is brewed up as a medicinal tisane for chill (OP 281–82), and in the second a strong black tea is prescribed as a hair darkener (NR 78). All manner of wild teas were experimented with on the plains, sometimes as a drink (never very popular) and sometimes as a medicine. Pungent and medicinal yarrow tea was brewed for cold sores, ulcers, and sore gums, and catnip tea, for example, was used to combat brain fever, whatever that was.

Milk does not get frequent mention in Cather, and in that regard she reflects the general situation of plains pioneer life. The difficulty of cooling milk accounts for that in part; I spent some time in Germany in the late 1950s, when refrigeration was still a luxury there, and I suspect the pattern there was much like that of the plains pioneers. We went to the market early in the morning to buy fresh milk and had a bit of it on hot cereal for breakfast. What was left was put on the window sill to clabber and we had it as a kind of pudding, *harte Milch,* with supper.

Cather mentions milk as a foodstuff several times without giving details for its application (OP 34, NR 92), and on two occasions it is depicted as the sort of thing a sick person drinks (MA 35, OO 125). Mrs. Shimerda uses milk on mush, much the same as we might use it today (MA 124), and canned milk is labeled as the kind of thing bachelor homesteaders use (MA 34) (for what, we are not told, but I suspect as a coffee emollient).

Little is said of buttermilk, but in *My Ántonia* (p. 51) the poor Shimerda family comes to the Burden house to get some. May we assume from this that it is a charity of what are essentially the leavings of the dairy process? Was it to be drunk or used in cooking? We cannot tell from Cather's text, but of course we can surmise that it might have been for both purposes. An interesting contrast is that between the buttermilk that results from beating cream or milk into butter and that which is produced by adding cultured bacteria to milk, the process which produces our modern "buttermilk." The pioneers of course made butter from their cream or whole milk and wound up with a whey called buttermilk, a substantially different product from the cultured buttermilk we can buy today.

I like cultured buttermilk, but I also like real buttermilk, which, I can assure you, is totally different from cultured buttermilk. The next time you pass a dairy farm that has a sign advertising whole milk, stop and pick up a gallon or two. Make it into butter (see the next section) and treat yourself and your family to a pioneer treat: real buttermilk.

Sweets and Treats

On the earliest frontier, candy was an unheard-of luxury; a bit of honey, maple sugar, or fruit leathers might be the only sweet a child ever saw. It is an idea usually met with amazement or even skepticism, but there were no honeybees on the pioneer plains; bees, in fact, are not native to America.

Sweets were always at a premium on the pioneer plains. Sugar was sold in "loaves," rock-hard cakes from which hunks were chipped off with heavy scissors-like pliers. During hard times few families could afford even loaf sugar. Few maple trees were to be found here, far too few to make tapping a practical solution to the problem. Box elder trees were tapped, however, and the sap boiled down into a passable sugar. Sorghum was used widely in recipes, in coffee, and on flapjacks. The use of sorghum that I enjoy most however is sorghum butter, spread on toast. It is simple enough to make—mix one part butter to one part sorghum molasses—but the result is a joy even to the modern palate.

One of the few candy recipes collected by the field workers of the WPA in the late 1930s is labeled in the files of the Nebraska State Historical Society "An excellent recipe," which makes it all the more worthwhile trying:

> Six cups of white sugar, one and a half of vinegar, one of molasses, and a teaspoonful of butter. Cook about forty minutes.

A natural candy was made in the form of "leathers," in which the natural sugars occurring in fruits and berries were concentrated by drying. Plums (the preferred type was the very sweet yellow wild plum), apricots, peaches, or other fruits were pitted and thoroughly mashed. The resultant puree was then slowly cooked down to a thick, sticky "butter." The slow evaporation of the moisture from the mixture concentrated the natural sugars. The butter was then spread on a tin and set in the sun (covered with a screen or flybar) or put in a slow oven until it had dried even more. The name of the confection describes its consistency well: leather. It served not only as a way of preserving fruits but also as one of the few sweets a pioneer child might have.

Cather's novels deal with the years of settlement. Just as there are bakeries and ice cream shops in her towns, there were also bees (OO 205) and commercial candies. The bulk of the references in her plains novels are to commercial boxed candies (OP 12, 13, 179; MA 4, 358).

The most pervasive function of candies in Cather's works is as a courting device. Again and again we see boxes of candy being presented as a courtship gift (above citations and OO 98). More than that, candy is shown as a symbol of affection, quite beyond courtship. Some of that symbolism is very tender:

"Poor Ole! He used to bring me candy from town, hidden in his feed-bag. He couldn't refuse anything to a girl. He'd have given away his tattoos long ago, if he could." (MA 283)

Interior of the Miner Store, Red Cloud, Nebraska

Rosicky's children look forward to a trip to town because of the potential for buying candy (NR 89), and he himself uses the occasion to buy sweets for his fine wife. His actions may not have been totally altruistic: after one shopping expedition he directs the grocer to give him his change in candy for the wife, and the clerk comments on his habit of always buying sweets for her, adding, "First thing you know, she'll be getting too fat." Rosicky gives an answer in keeping with his eastern European peasant tradition, "I'd like dat. I ain't much fur all dem slim women like what de style is now" (NR 80). Perhaps the more modern feminine counterpart to that exchange occurs in *My Ántonia*; Lena, when passing a candy store would slow her pace and murmur,

"Get me by if you can." She was very fond of sweets, and was afraid of growing too plump. (MA 280)

Commercial candies like cinnamon drops were used to decorate other products from the oven, such as gingerbread men (MA 81), and peppermints served, as they do now, as balm for a cough-irritated throat (OO 53).

Taffy was a favorite pioneer candy because it was a standard for kitchen courtship: for the couple it gave the modest opportunity to touch hands—accidentally, of course—while pulling the confection; for the family in the parlor it provided the comforting thought that the young peoples' hands were too busy and too sticky for anything more serious than those serendipitous touches. Taffy is a commonly encountered homemade candy in Cather's plains novels (MA 67, 176, 180).

The following is a handwritten note that had been inserted between the pages of the Cathers' *Home Queen Cook Book*:

2 cups of sugar, 1 quart new milk, 1 quart cream, 1–2 cups of flour (scant) 1 tablespoon vanilla; put 1 cup of sugar in a skillet and let it melt slowly, stirring constantly and boil until it becomes a brown syrup, then pour into the milk and when it boils the caramel will have dissolved (this is to be cooked in a double boiler); beat together 3 eggs, then 1–2 cups flour and other cup of sugar, stir into the boiling mixture, let boil, stirring all the while, set aside to cool and when cold beat in the cream, add vanilla and freeze; when nearly frozen add 1 cup chopped English walnuts. Mrs. N. M. Doudna

The next recipe, for cream candy, is from a handwritten note inserted in Mrs. Lea's *Domestic Cookery,* and it has been a major detective problem in the compilation of this collection. The writing is virtually illegible and the recipe is stained and worn, indicating that it was a popular family recipe. Linda managed to pry out the bulk of the information from the tattered slip of paper, but we must apologize for the gaps that remain in the recipe:

1 cup granulated sugar with three tablespoonsful of cream. Put in a porcelan [*sic*] kettle   let it dissolve on back of the stove. Thin [or perhaps *then*] set it forward let it boil until crisp in water [hard-ball test] Stir in a teaspoonfull of rose, vanilla or any extract. Pour out and when cool pull. Cut in squares.

The following recipes for chocolate fudge and cream fudge are from Marion Howland's article in *Woman's World*:

Two cups granulated sugar, one cup of milk, one-half cake of sweet chocolate, small piece of butter, vanilla to flavor. Let boil eight minutes, then beat to a cream and put into buttered pans to cool.

Three cups of a soft A [*sic*] sugar, one cup of milk, small piece of butter and flavor to taste. Boil ten minutes, beat to a cream and cool in buttered pans.

A handwritten recipe for divinity was found in the pages of *The White House Cook Book*:

3 cups sugar
1 cup corn syrup
1 cup boiling water
Boil together until it threads VERY good.
Cool by stirring for five minutes. Then add the beaten whites of three eggs. Put in half pound shelled nuts the last thing.

Popped corn and taffy are mentioned in the same sentence in *My Ántonia* (p. 67) as the sort of foundation one might have for a standard pioneer evening entertainment. And of course taffy (in a syrup form) and popcorn could be combined in popcorn balls (MA 159). Popcorn was also sold commercially on the streets of Cather's towns (MA 195) and was used for Christmas decoration as well as for a snack food (MA 82).

Pies were a standard pioneer dessert, made from wild berries like gooseberries and sand cherries and from domestic garden plants like rhubarb and apples. All manner of produce, but most notably apples, was dried to be used in pies later in the winter. Apples were cored, sliced, strung on cords and hung in festoons about the house to dry. I am sure dried-apple pies were a pleasant relief from the sometimes monotonous pioneer diet, but there are also suggestions that they fell short of being gourmet fare. The following passage from *A Treasury of Nebraska Pioneer Folklore* (p. 310) is probably representative:

Charles Miller, who lived in Thayer County during the 1870s, says he always thinks of dried apples when pioneer fare is mentioned. A meal of water and dried apples made him feel as if he was moving through the air in a toy balloon. But the dried apples, for many, were unsavory food. They were tough, leathery, dirty-brown in color, and nearly always fly-specked. One settler in Gage County described them in this ditty:

Spit in my ears and tell me lies,
But give me no dried apple pies.

The pie that always seemed to me to capture the essence of life and hopes on the Nebraska plains was variously labeled Mock-Apple Pie, Transparent Pie, or Cracker Pie. It was an effort to have good old American apple pie out on the Great American Desert, where there were no good old American apples.

A popular brand of party cracker still carries a recipe for mock apple pie, but perhaps we should note that the modern soda cracker, saltine, or party cracker has little in common with the pioneer cracker, which was more like a ship's biscuit. Pioneers crackers measured three to five inches square and a half-inch to an inch thick. Most notably they were hard as rocks (which contributed to their durability under poor storage conditions) and required soaking before they could be put to any use other than building chimneys. This version of the pie recipe is from the *Dakota City* (Nebraska) *Mail* of May 22, 1874:

Take six soda crackers. Break them in a dish and pour over them two cups of cold water. Let them stand until they can be reduced to a pulp. One and one-half cups of sugar, two teaspoons of tartaric acid, and flavor to taste with lemon. This is sufficient for two pies.

And yet another version from the January, 1877, *Nebraska Farmer*:

Break in pieces one and one-half crackers and pour over them a cup of cold water; let it stand while making the paste. Put in a pie plate with a little nutmeg, add a cup of sugar and the juice of one lemon, vinegar may do.

By now it must be evident that the pioneer cook continued to make her pies and cakes, but all manner of adjustments were necessary because of a restricted cupboard inventory. It was make do or do without. Another pie that might be found in almost any soddie was Buttermilk Pie. This version is from the Hueftle family near Eustis:

 1 cup sugar
 1 teaspoon butter
 1½ cups buttermilk
 1 egg
 1 tablespoon flour
 Stir well together, flavor with nutmeg. Bake in one crust like custard pie.

From the same pioneer family comes a cake recipe that boasts the imposing name Thrashers' Cup:

 3 cups sugar
 2 cups sweet cream
 4 eggs (beaten)
 1 cup sweet milk
 salt—vanilla
 4 cups flour
 5 teaspoons baking powder
 nuts
 Makes 3 dozen.

The most popular dessert offered up from Cather's kitchens is pie, so common on the American scene, so typical of the frontier table. There are apple pies (OO 56), pumpkin pies (MA 19), and prune pies (OP 28), but there are also simply pies, frequently shown as they are produced in pioneer kitchens in a factory-like process (OP 85, 241; OO 138). Materials from the sections of this book on gardens and orchards surely also speak to the issue of pies, for we find trees bent with cherries, apples, and peaches, rhubarb and ground-cherries, and raspberries, all materials suitable for pies.

The Cather files contain many manuscript and printed recipes for pies clearly marked as favorites. The following cream pie is from *The Home Queen Cook Book* (p. 392), where it is circled and labeled "fine":

Boil 1½ pts. milk and add to it 3 table-spoons corn starch dissolved in a little milk, 1 cup sugar and butter the size of a small egg. Pour this mixture over the beaten yolks of 3 eggs, and add lemon extract or flavoring of some kind to taste. Pour this into the pie-plates lined with paste, and bake about 20 minutes. Beat the whites of the 3 eggs with a little sugar, spread over the pie, and brown lightly in the oven.

This recipe for cream pie is a typewritten note—on State Bank of Red Cloud letterhead—found in the pages of the Cathers' *Home Queen Cook Book*:

1½ cups sugar, yolks of six eggs, stir well, then add six tablespoons of flour, stir well,

4½ cups of milk (let it boil in double boiler) add three tablespoons of butter to the boiling milk.

Then stir sugar, eggs, and flour in slowly. Flavor to taste and frost with the whites of six eggs.

A handwritten note in the pages of the Cathers' *White House Cook Book* provides a recipe for banana pie:

Make a shell. When cool slice into it two bananas.

⅔ cup sugar

1 cup milk

1 teaspoon butter

Let this boil up well then add to it a little salt and flour enough to thicken—about one tablespoonful.

Use whites of two eggs for the top and brown it.

I used whipped cream the last time instead of egg whites & it was so good.

This recipe for lemon pie had been cut from *Home Circle* and was found in the pages of the Cathers' *Home Queen Cook Book*:

For one pie take the juice and grated rind (do not use the white part of the rind); grate off the yellow of 1 lemon; beat 2 eggs; add 1 cup of sugar and mix in the lemon juice and rind; then take 2 teaspoonfuls of corn starch dissolved in a little cold water and add to 1 pint of boiling water, stirring until thick and clear. Mix all together, line a deep pie plate with pie crust and put in the filling.

This handwritten lemon pie recipe found in *The White House Cook Book* carried the title "Jessie receipt for lemon pie":

1 lemon
1 egg yolks [*sic*]
1 cup sugar
1 table spoonful of corn starch [*sic*]
1 cup of hot water
Frost the top of the pie with the whites of the two eggs.

Lemon pie must have been a Cather family favorite. This one, handwritten, was found in *The White House Cook Book*:

Yolks of 4 eggs
whites " 1 egg
2 tbs flour
½ cup water
¾ " sugar
1 lemon
Top whites of 3 eggs, 4 tablespoons of sugar

From Sally Hotovy's kitchen comes this recipe for Deep Dish Apple Pie:

1½ c. flour
¼ t. salt
½ c. shortening
¼ c. milk
Cut shortening into flour and salt mixture. Add milk—blend. (Do not work dough too hard. This makes crust tough.) Roll into 2 crusts one slightly larger. Use larger for bottom crust in 9″ by 9″ square pan.
Slice apples (4 cups?). Alternate layers of sliced apples & sugar mixture of ⅔ c. sugar, 1 teas cinn, pinch of salt & 3 T. flour.
Place top crust on, pinching and sealing the 2 crust edges together. Poke several holes in top with fork & sprinkle with sugar. Bake 50 min to 1 hr or until top is Brown.
Bake at 400°.

And from Alice Styskal come recipes for pie crust and cherry pie:

Take one cup of lard, a quart of sifted flour and a pinch of salt. Work together and add only enough cold water to make dough stick together. Roll in one direction. This will make two pies or four without upper crust. For a richer crust, mix a cup of lard, a cup of butter and a quart of flour, two egg yolks and a pinch of salt. Then add water to hold dough together.

Pit your cherries and sprinkle with sugar, dust with flour and fill a lined pie plate with them. Most fruit pies are made this way. The amount of sugar depends on the acidity of the fruit. Cover with crust and bake.

The Cather family recipe files have several cookie recipes that are clearly marked as favorites. The first, for gingersnaps, is from an undated, untitled newspaper clipping found in the family's *White House Cook Book*:

One cup each of molasses, sugar and shortening, one-half cup hot water, teaspoonful of soda dissolved in this, teaspoonful of ginger, allspice, clove and grated nutmeg, a pinch of salt, and one egg. Add flour to roll, bake in a quick oven. Mary Froehlich.

Another gingersnap recipe was cut from *Demorest's Monthly Magazine* and is undated. It was found in the pages of *The Home Queen Cook Book*:

Butter . . . one-half coffee cup
Lard . . .   "   "
Sugar . . . one   "
Molasses . . . "   "
Water . . . one-half   "
Ginger . . . one tablespoonful
Cinnamon . . . "   "
Cloves . . .   "   teaspoonful
Soda . . .   "   "
Flour . . . to roll
Roll, thin, and bake quickly.

The ginger cookies recipe below was handwritten on a card found in *The White House Cook Book*:

1½ cups of molasses
½ cup G. Sugar

1 cup S. cream
1 egg
1 teas heaping full of soda ginger and spice at least
1 cup of butter or lard
Bake in a hot oven

On the same card is written this recipe for "bakers cookies":

2 cups of molasses
½ cup sugar
1 cup of B milk or S cream
1 cup of shortening
1 teas of soda
1 tsp of cinnamon
2 of ginger
mix at night good and in morning and later wash the top with an egg
and molasses beaten together.

Eggs and dairy products, like potatoes and squash, may not
seem like a natural union, but Cather certainly treats them that way.
(In all honesty however I must note that in a letter dated February
20, 1943, Cather writes that she does not like eggs and never did.) It
is not simply a matter of the roles of the two items in food preparation but involves their relationship in family economics. Farming
tends to be a matter of famine or feast, there being unlikely vast
amounts of money when a crop or steer is sold but nothing on a
week-to-week basis.

Except for eggs, butter, and cream. This was considered to be
the money of the woman of the farm, and with its steady trickle she
could keep the household running on a fairly even keel. It was also
from this money that she could save a little here and there for special
things and special occasions, from a new Bible to a child's college
education. In his dying words Alexandra's father tells her brothers
that she can earn more selling her eggs and butter than a man can
earn in wages (OP 27), and his comfort while he lived was that the
hens were bringing in enough money to keep the family going
through the winter (OP 16).

In "Neighbour Rosicky" the Fassler family is criticized for

selling cream while depriving the children of nourishment. Says Mary (based on Anna Pavelka, Cather's model for Ántonia):

"Yes, . . . and look at them Fassler children! Pale, pinched little things, they look like skimmed milk. I had rather put some colour into my children's faces than put money into the bank." (NR 84)

Eggs are eggs, and while a woman might take pride in the quality of her chickens, the product was still a matter of the chickens. She might be noted for having clean eggs or lots of eggs or carefully graded eggs, but the manufacturing was by and large out of her hands. It should perhaps be noted however that Enid Wheeler did take pride in the purity of her hens' strain, fretting about their being mixed with Plymouth Rocks and therefore depriving them of the attention of a rooster, even as she was in the process of abandoning her husband (OO 190).

Butter was another matter. The housewife made her butter and she sold it and she took ferocious pride in it. It had to be clean and free of buttermilk. It was carefully molded in wooden forms. Sometimes the mold had in it a mark that was a woman's distinctive trademark; other women scratched or pressed a distinctive mark into their butter so that the buyer would know whose product it was. For family use, butter might be kept more simply, perhaps in a jar (MA 19).

Butter is easily made. Pavel made his own butter from his own cow's milk, "beating sour cream with a wooden spoon" (MA 35). Pioneer-style butter can be made by placing whole, unhomogenized cream or milk in a jar with plenty of empty space and simply shaking it gently for a quarter-hour or so. Or it can be beaten with a spoon or worked gently and slowly with a beater. It will seem as if the process is going nowhere and then suddenly the butter will come, as the pioneers said. Quite remarkably, here all at once are clumps of butter in the milk, which has now become buttermilk.

The pioneer housewife pushed the clots of butter together with a wooden spoon or paddle and then kneaded it until every bead of buttermilk had been worked out of it. The butter is then washed in cold water and is again worked clean of residual moisture.

This was the pioneer child's chore, and even today it can be a great exercise in pioneer living for modern children on a rainy fall or spring day. The real reward of course is at the kitchen table.

There were all manner of rotary, manufactured wooden churns, but they were expensive and difficult to keep in running condition. The pioneer housewife usually had a smaller churn: a one-gallon glass jar with a lid incorporating a churn paddle and turning handle, or a crock churn holding five to fifteen gallons with a wooden lid and dasher that was worked up and down (OP 149, MA 355). Working a dasher through five gallons of cream was a real job. And the woman who could keep her family in butter and have some left to sell in town was recognized as a resource who ensured the survival of her family:

"Mary Svoboda's the best butter-maker in all this country, and a fine manager. Her children will have a grand chance. (MA 349)

Eggs and butter were blended in a rare condiment, mayonnaise, but one which is mentioned as being the product of one of the fanciest cooks recognized in the community, the sort of cook who excelled at church suppers but whose husband chose to eat at the hotel in town. With that warning, we will include recipes for mayonnaise as provided by Berniece Pelt, who is skilled at all levels of cookery, humble and fancy:

Mix ½ cup sugar
3 teaspoons salt
2 teaspoons mustard
Add: 2 cups sour cream
1 cup vinegar and 4 eggs
Cook in a double boiler until thick.

1 egg yolk
2 tsp sugar
2 tbsp vinegar or lemon juice or tbsp each
1 cup salad oil
¼ tsp mustard
½ tsp salt
Beat yolk until stiff, add oil, ½ tsp at a time. Keep beating. Add oil

in larger amounts when dressing thickens. Pickles, olives, celery, or pimento may be added if desired. Add paprika to color. (Salad oil was probably olive oil.)

Another dairy-poultry combination is mentioned in *One of Ours* in a context that also explains why cookery is folklore: its transmission is primarily by informal means:

Gladys was in the kitchen, . . . looking for her mother's glasses,—mislaid when she was copying a recipe for a cheese soufflé. (OO 93)

In my own research I have encountered little mention of cheese on the plains frontier. The severity of summers may account for that. Cather mentions cheese twice in her plains novels, and in both cases the cheeses are imported, in the one instance rather explicitly as the sort of thing one found in the cities but not the countryside (MA 217, OO 32–33).

Mrs. R. I. Cooper's recipe for a real country cheese was submitted to us by her daughter Mary Lambrecht, who notes, "This never aged at our house. Great on fresh bread":

Cook 6 quarts of thick clabber milk over a slow fire as for cottage cheese. When a curd, mashed between the thumb and finger, retains its shape, pour into a cloth sack and hang on the clothes line to drain for 2 hours. Press out all possible moisture. In a double boiler, melt ½ pound of firm butter, 1 teaspoon soda, 2 teaspoon salt. When melted add the cottage cheese, cook until melted soft. The butter and cheese will be separated until the cream is added. This will take an hour or longer for the cheese to get soft. Then add 1 pint thick sour cream to which a small amount of cheese coloring (yellow) has been added. Beat until thick, then mold in a small bread pan. This makes 2½ pounds. It is ready to use at once but improves with age.

I was reminded of my own small-town, backwoods, rural nature when I received a long-distance call from a researcher for the Disney movie studio. The studio, he told me, was producing a new television series that would explore various people, processes, and items that seem to have been lost in time. The staff hoped to find age-old skills that most people presumed were lost years ago but which still might survive in hidden pockets—like latter-day dinosaurs. I thought I understood that thesis well enough, and I said I could perhaps help. I know of some homesteaders and some surviving soddies and log houses, and I know Omaha Indians who still know the old songs and stories. But I decided it just might not be worth the effort when the eager and excited researcher told me that the studio was well into production of the first program and already had filmed a remarkable family in Boston who actually pack ice and milk and salt and sugar into a complicated bucket system, turn a handle for what seems like forever and wind up with—*ice cream!* Could I believe that? he asked. I allowed as how I could.

Cather's nineteenth-century plains villages, virtually on the edge of the frontier in history and geography, nonetheless already had ice cream parlors, and as often as not that is the context for ice cream in her novels (MA 196, 215; NR 92) and the context for her young people's social lives. Marie Shabata apparently considered the making of ice cream to be part of social courtesy, for Alexandra fears telling her that she is coming for a visit, lest Marie set to baking cakes and freezing ice cream:

"She'll always make a party if you give her the least excuse." (OP 133)

The following newspaper clipping, titled only "The best way to make ice cream" and dated only August 12, was found between the pages of *The Home Queen Cook Book*:

Where cream alone is used in making ice cream one-half or one-third of the quantity used should be scalded, the sugar dissolved in the scalded portion, and when cool added to the remaining quantity of cream. Where cream is not obtainable, milk may be used enriched by the yolks of eggs, allowing four to each quart of milk. Scald the milk in a double boiler; beat the eggs and sugar together; add to the hot milk, cook for a moment then strain into the ice cream mold and freeze.

PEACH

One quart cream, one pint milk, two cups sugar, white of two eggs, one dozen ripe peaches. Pare and mash the peaches, add sugar, and let it stand; add cream and milk and just before freezing the beaten whites.

VANILLA

One quart of cream, one pint of milk, two cups of sugar, whites of two eggs, one teaspoonful of vanilla. Mix the sugar with the cream and milk; add flavoring and strain into freezer. Beat the whites to a stiff froth and add just before freezing.

This ice cream recipe is from a handwritten note found between the pages of the Cathers' *White House Cook Book*:

Beat 4 eggs well, mix
1 tablespoon sugar with
1 tablespoon cornstarch
Bring to a boil
1 qt. of milk.
Stir in eggs, sugar and cornstarch and cook. Let cool and stir in 2 qts milk. Sweet to suit taste with Karo and [unidentifiable word that looks like *Frupe* underlined. Foreign word? Commercial name?]

Homemade ice cream is a remarkable surprise for anyone accustomed to commercial ice cream—as is the case with almost all foodstuffs. But as is the case too with butter, the making of ice cream (and the licking of the dasher) are most appropriately the activities set aside for children, for never is the direct relationship between labor and reward more obvious. I suspect that America could be set aright again if the government would give each newborn child an ice cream bucket with a hand-turned crank.

Enid, the generally unsatisfactory wife, makes puddings (oo 190), and they are therefore to be suspected. Things that are cooked because they are "good for us" are usually not good at all. On the other hand, Jim Burden refers to his grandmother's pudding as his favorite, "striped with currants and boiled in a bag" (MA 66).

The following recipe for cornstarch pudding had been cut from an undated, untitled, and otherwise unidentified newspaper and glued inside the end boards of the Cathers' copy of Mrs. Lea's *Domestic Cookery*:

Beat the whites of three eggs to a stiff froth. Dissolve two tablespoonfuls of corn starch in a little cold milk saved from a pint, which is the quantity needed for this pudding. Stir a level half tea-cupful of sugar and a pinch of salt in the remainder of the pint, and put the whole in a double kettle over the fire. When it comes to a boil, stir in the corn starch previously dissolved; and stir constantly for a few moments, when it will become a perfectly smooth paste. Now add the beaten whites of the eggs and stir two or three moments longer until these are cooked. Flavor with vanilla, and then pour into mold, which you have previously wet with cold water.

Make a custard with the yolks of the eggs, half a cupful of sugar and a pint of milk, pour over the pudding. Very good.

A bag-pudding recipe from an untitled newspaper clipping was found inserted between the pages of the Cathers' *Home Queen Cook Book*:

One cup of currants, one cup of seedless raisins, one cup of suet chopped fine, one cup of milk, one cup of molasses, three cups of flour, two teaspoonfuls of baking powder. Place in a pudding bag, allowing room for it to swell. Put into a kettle of fast-boiling water and boil for three hours. It may be kept on hand and steamed when wanted.

From page 94 of Mrs. Lea's *Domestic Cookery*:

Bread pudding is made out of bread that is too dry to use; cut it fine, boil it in milk, and mash it well, beat four eggs and put in, with half a pound of raisins; boil it an hour and a half, or bake it.

The following three recipes, for Bread and Apple Pudding ("to be eaten with a sauce"), Custard Hasty Pudding, and Baked Pudding are from pages 94 and 95 of Mrs. Lea's *Domestic Cookery*:

Put a layer of buttered bread in the bottom of a well buttered dish, with chopped apples, sugar, grated bread and butter, and a little pounded cinnamon; fill up the dish with alternate layers of these articles, observing that it is better to have the inner layer of bread thinner than that of the top and bottom. This is a nice dish for those who cannot partake of pastry.

Put a quart of new milk on to boil; then mix a teacup of rice flour with a little milk, two eggs; and three spoonsful of sugar; beat it, and when your milk boils, stir it in; let it boil five minutes—then pour it out on some buttered toast, in a bowl or dish, and grate nutmeg over it.

Boil a quart of milk, and stir into it half a pint of corn meal and a tea-spoonful of salt—mix this well together; beat two eggs, stir in when nearly cold; add a tea-cup of chopped suet, two table-spoonsful of sugar, a little spice—grease a pan, and pour it in; bake three-quarters of an hour. Eat it with sugar and cream, or molasses sauce.

Suet pudding appears from its numbers in the Cather files to be a special favorite of the family, although it is not mentioned in Cather's works. The following suet pudding recipe is from an undated and untitled newspaper clipping circled, marked with an X, and found between the pages of *The Home Queen Cook Book*:

To one teacupful of finely chopped suet add four cups of flour that have been sifted with a teaspoonful of baking powder. Add a half-pound of raisins, a cup of molasses, a cup of milk and a pinch of salt. Flavor with cinnamon, boil two and a half hours and serve with sauce.

Jennie Miner Reiher, a cousin of Willa Cather, contributed the next suet-pudding recipe:

1⅓ C. suet chopped fine
½ c. brown sugar
½ c. molasses
1 c. sour milk
1 cup raisins
2½ c. flour to 3½ cups
2 eggs
1 tsp soda
1 tsp cloves
1 tsp cinnamon
Pinch nutmeg and salt
Steam 3 hours, may add currants, nuts, and citron and a few dry bread crumbs.

SWEET PUDDING SAUCE:
Mix together
1 c sugar (half white and half brown)
2 T Corn starch (or flour)
Stir in gradually
2 cups boiling water

Boil 1 minute stirring constantly
Add
4 tablespoons butter
2 tsp of lemon juice or vinegar or vanilla
1 tsp nutmeg
Pinch salt

The following recipe for English Plum Pudding ("The Original") is from page 377 of *The White House Cook Book,* as is also the second recipe, Christmas Plum Pudding ("By Measure"):

Soak one pound of stale bread in a pint of hot milk and let it stand and cool. When cold, add to it one-half pound of sugar and the yolks of eight eggs beaten to a cream, one pound of raisins, stoned [*sic*] and floured, one pound of Sante [*sic*] currants, washed and floured, a quarter of a pound of citron cut in slips and dredged with flour, one pound of beef suet, chopped fine and salted, one glass of wine, one glass of brandy, one nutmeg and a tablespoonful of mace, cinnamon and cloves mixed; beat the whole well together and, as the last thing, add the whites of the eight eggs, beaten to a stiff froth; pour into a cloth, previously scaled and dredged with flour, tie it firmly, leaving room for the pudding to swell and boil six hours. Serve with wine or brandy sauce.

It is best to prepare the ingredients the day before and cover closely.

One cupful of finely-chopped beef suet, two cupfuls of fine bread crumbs, one heaping cupful of sugar, one cupful of seeded raisins, one cupful of well-washed currants, one cupful of chopped blanched almonds, half a cupful of citron sliced thin, a teaspoonful of salt, one of cloves, two of cinnamon, half a grated nutmeg and four well-beaten eggs. Dissolve a level teaspoonful of soda in a tablespoonful of warm water. Flour the fruit thoroughly from a pint of flour; then mix the remainder as follows: in a large bowl put the well-beaten eggs, sugar, spices, and salt in one cupful of milk. Stir in the fruit, chopped nuts, bread crumbs and suet, one after the other, until all are used, putting in the dissolved soda last and adding enough flour to make the fruit stick together, which will take all the pint. Boil or steam four hours. Serve with wine or brandy or any well-flavored sauce.

This recipe for boiled pudding is from the Cathers' *Home Queen Cook Book* (p. 445), where it is circled, marked with an X, and twice labeled "good":

One cup milk, 1 cup suet. Make fine 1 lb. raisins, 1 lb. currants, 1 small tea-spoon soda, a salt-spoon of salt, citron if you like it, flour to make a stiff batter, 1 cup molasses. Put the soda into the molasses and beat it to a froth, then put all together and stir well. Boil from 2 to 3 hours. Eat with sauce.

Sauce for boiled pudding—one cup sugar, 1 egg, piece of butter size of a walnut, 1 table-spoon flour. Beat all together into 1 pt. boiling milk, flavor with brandy or wine.

And finally a plum-pudding recipe from the Cathers' *Home Queen Cook Book* (p. 454):

Four cups flour, 2 eggs, 1 very large cup brown sugar; 1 table-spoon butter, 1 tea-spoon cinnamon, 2 tea-spoons baking powder, 1 cup milk, 1 cup seeded raisins, a pinch of salt; beat eggs very light, add sugar, butter, milk, raisins, and beat as each ingredient is added; flour, baking powder, and cinnamon sifted together, bake in buttered dish 1 hour in slow oven. Serve hot with vanilla sauce. When cold is a good fruit cake.

OR

Take 1 lb. raisins, same of currants, same of suet, chop the latter very fine, ½ lb. sour apples chopped, 1 lb. flour, 6 eggs, ½ cup citron chopped fine, 3 wine-glasses unfermented wine, 1 lb. brown sugar, spice to taste. If too dry, add sweet milk. Tie tightly in a pudding bag, well floured and boil 4½ hours.

Herbs and Seasonings

Very little is made of seasonings and herbs in Cather's works. There is mention in *One of Ours* (p. 221) of a mint bed, but we are not told whether the leaves were used to flavor drinks or jellies or merely sweetened the summer breezes. In *O Pioneers!* (p. 134) the herb rosemary is mentioned, but only as the basis for a sachet to keep stored clothing smelling sweet.

The herb most frequently mentioned is tobacco. In *O Pioneers!* (p. 22) Cather notes that many of the migrants to the plains had not been farmers in the Old Country but *handwerkers,* such as cigar makers. In those days tobacco was often shipped in bulk to small-town entrepreneurs, who made a cottage industry of producing hand-rolled and pressed cigars. Just as the men bought candy in town for their wives and children, they also bought tobacco for themselves (OP 13), often taking it in a pipe before or after supper (MA 48). When Doctor Burleigh admits that he cannot imagine successfully persuading Rosicky to drink less coffee, he includes the other Bohemian vice too:

"I've never yet been able to separate a Bohemian from his coffee or his pipe." (NR 73)

Cather usually associates tobacco with voluptuous contentment, from Cuzak's joy with his family situation (MA 366) to Claude Wheeler's evening pipe, taken outdoors because his mother will not allow him to smoke inside (OO 67). Cigarettes are mentioned only once, but in the same context of contentment (MA 260), and as Cather so often does, contrary characters are developed as much by what they avoid as by what they embrace:

Cutter . . . said he got his start in life by saving the money that other young men spent for cigars. He was full of moral maxims for boys. (MA 209)

Perhaps the closest we can come to experiencing frontier tobaccos is to sample twists of bulk tobacco such as one can sometimes purchase in tobacco-producing regions like Kentucky. The harsh molasses-cured twists were often crushed and mixed with stretchers, which like those used in coffees of the period not only helped save money but also mellowed the strength of the product. Tobacco on the plains was stretched with sumac, garden-grown tobacco, mullein, and shavings from pear, apricot, or apple trees. Tobacco was often a part of the pioneer garden. We tend to think today of tobacco as a southern product, forgetting that a major tobacco-producing region of America is Wisconsin.

Conclusions

For this book we have drawn from *My Ántonia, O Pioneers!,
One of Ours,* and "Neighbour Rosicky," but there is ample reason to
believe that our conclusions can be carried well beyond that limited
bibliography. The reader can turn to Cather's "The Best Years"
(*Five Stories,* pp. 124–25) and find a meal that might just as well be
found in *One of Ours* or *O Pioneers!*:

"I'll scramble you an egg and fry you some ham, so sit right down in your
own place. I have some stewed plums for your dessert, and a beautiful angel
cake I bought at the Methodist bake sale." . . .

Mrs. Ferguson brought the ham and eggs and the warmed-up coffee.
Then she sat down opposite her daughter to watch her enjoy her supper.
"Now don't talk to her, boys. Let her eat in peace."

Lucy Gayheart (New York: Alfred A. Knopf, 1936) contains
passages that echo the Cather foods and attitudes toward foods we
have treated here: hunting (pp. 189, 223), whiskey and tobacco (pp.
6, 9, 209), cottage cheese (p. 192), church dinners (p. 190), cakes
(pp. 176, 182), coffee (pp. 161, 176), candies (p. 171), eggs (p. 161),
orchards (pp. 155, 156), and Bohemians and their beer (p. 151).

A Lost Lady (New York: Random House, 1972) is usually seen
as a plains novel, but the principal family, the Forresters, enjoy a
cosmopolitan lifestyle, even at Sweet Water. There are still the hints
at the peasant and pioneer foods that characterize Cather's other
plains novels—the cookies of the household's Bohemian cook (pp.

16, 18), the rye bread (p. 17), sausages (p. 17), cheeses (p. 17), game (pp. 22, 66, 68, 71, 163), and catfish (pp. 68, 163) of the frontier—but the action of the novel takes place within a family that enjoys an elegant board. The result is a foodways inventory that is typical of an elite social class rather than of a historic time (the frontier) or region (the Great Plains)—barrels of eastern bourbon (pp. 34, 35, 104), a cellar full of claret (p. 80), cocktails (pp. 45, 46, 158), sherry from decanters (pp. 38, 96), port (p. 96), teas and toast (pp. 39, 74, 146), maraschino cherries (p. 47), salads and frozen pudding (p. 162)—all "properly placed" (p. 48). As opposed to the unself-conscious use of foods by the traditional pioneer family ("We eat what we eat"), the Forresters' noblesse oblige requires them to consider carefully a maintenance of their standards: "A gentleman had such books in his library, just as he had claret in his cellar" (p. 81).

Cather nonetheless manipulates food as a motif within the novel to point out precisely this contrast. Foods in Cather's works are never employed casually or superficially. When the boys from town come to eat at the elegant Forrester table, they do not know how to hold their cocktail glasses (p. 160). The sophistication of the meal is lost on them, for "a beefsteak with potatoes would have pleased them better! They didn't really like this kind of food at all." (p. 162).

When the Forrester household is in a state of collapse and the ordinary citizens from the town come to see the wonders of the home, the contrast becomes even more explicit. The visitors look upon the tools of elegant dining and imagine how they would adapt them for their own more humble tables: champagne glasses, perhaps, to serve sherbet in, long-stemmed goblets for mantel ornaments, unsuitable for any "normal" use, "unless she can get the saloons to take 'em" (p. 139). In *A Lost Lady,* Cather draws attention to the nature of pioneer plains foods by showing the reader their antithesis.

Cather's intense use of foodways as a literary motif, her skillful observations of pioneer and ethnic foodways, and her recollection of foods from her own family's kitchen are, we may therefore assume, not characteristics unique to the works we have used in this study. Indeed, her experiences in food and her understanding of its vital role in plains pioneer culture (any culture for that matter) is not hers alone. We will explore in future volumes plains pioneer food-ways motifs as they were used by other authors. We have started with Cather for the very sound reason that she was so marvelously good at it.

Index

This index is a guide only to food references and recipes. The recipes are signaled by italic page numbers. Foods are listed here by the names they appear under in Cather's writing. Individual ingredients in recipes are not indexed.